Ketogenic Diet for 50 Plus

How To the Ketogenic Diet Can Help To Boost Your Weight Loss, Reboot Metabolism and Get Healthy Without Meds and Gym Easy-To-Follow 30-Day Diet Plan

By

Leonard Diesen

The information herein is offered for informational purposes solely, and is universal as so. The presentation of the information is without contract or any type of guarantee assurance.

The trademarks that are used are without any consent, and the publication of the trademark is without permission or backing by the trademark owner. All trademarks and brands within this book are for clarifying purposes only and are the owned by the owners themselves, not affiliated with this document.

Table of content

Introduction

The ketogenic diet is an eating style that consists of very high fat, medium protein, and low carbohydrate macronutrient ratios to encourage a ketosis state in the body. Ketosis occurs when the body is depleted from glucose, and glycogen is stored, which causes it to turn its metabolic pathways to start using fat as fuel. The body creates ketones as it begins to break down fats into fatty acids and is a message from the body to start to use both dietary & body fat as the main energy source. This is the natural source of energy for the body and something that is an inherent function of us all and helps our body to operate more effectively and efficiently. More importantly, there isn't a dependence on getting energy on the next meal. Ketones are the central focus of the ketogenic diet. Your body creates ketones, an energy molecule, like that of an alternate source of energy whenever the body runs low on blood sugar. Ketones are created when you lower the carb intake and eat just the right amounts of protein. Ketosis has been around for quite a long time and emerged as an epileptic medical intervention. Studies are now breaking out, showing their effectiveness in the treatment and reversal of diabetes, insulin resistance, anxiety, PCOS, obesity, as well as Alzheimer's disease. Yet more work is being done on this low carb lifestyle also for a "healthy" person, with excellent results and incredibly low risks. Whenever the body is in ketosis, this metabolic state allows the body, particularly for the brain, to have large quantities of energy ready.

There are a number of ways in which ketosis can be brought about, and therefore there are a number of different variants of the ketogenic diet. When on a keto diet, glycogen stores can always be refilled.

A ketogenic diet is an ideal way to create muscle, but this is where protein consumption is essential. It's proposed that you can take in around 1.0–1.2 grams of protein every lean pound of body mass if you're trying to add muscle. On a ketogenic diet, a growing muscle can be slower, but that's because the total body fat doesn't develop as fast. If you do need to add on body fat for whatever reason, you can accomplish your goals by different forms of a Keto diet. These are the famous variations of the keto diet: Standard Ketogenic Diet (SKD), Cyclical Ketogenic Diet (CKD), and Targeted Ketogenic Diet (TKD). Each serves a function unique to particular groups of individuals. You'll gain from one type more than the others, based on your objectives, your fitness routine, and your workout experience. The majority of studies suggest that the keto diet is more effective at helping you lose the weight & shed body fat than traditional diets. A number of studies say low-carb diets are similar to low-fat diets to make you lose weight in the long run. A ketogenic diet followed by daily physical exercise and wise food choices, such as consuming more low carb vegetables & fatty fish, improves its effectiveness in losing extra weight and fat. If you start a ketogenic diet, it's crucial to understand how to build your meals so you can eat a balanced balance of carbs, fats, and protein. Snacks are an easy thing to add to your keto diet menu; they do not have to be complex, and they're a way of adding healthy fats to your diet without raising your carbohydrate count. If you are a female over the age of 50, you can be even more interested in weight loss than you were at 30. A lot of women undergo a slowing metabolism at a rate of about 50 calories a day at this age. Assuming you don't suffer from health problems, a keto diet can bring many benefits, particularly in terms of weight loss. Eating a perfect mix of greens, lean meat, and unprocessed carbs is the most important consideration. Simply sticking to whole foods is perhaps the most successful way to eat healthily, mostly because it's a nutritious strategy. Slowing metabolism combined with less exercise, muscle degeneration as well as the potential for intensified cravings can make weight gain management extremely difficult. Many diet options are available to support weight loss, but the keto diet is among the most famous in recent years. The recipes elaborated later in the book are attached in a PDF file that'll help you in adopting the healthy lifestyle.

Chapter 1: Introduction to ketogenic diet

Despite continued advances in the medical field, obesity remains a major health hazard worldwide, with adult death as high as 2.8 million per annum. Many chronic illnesses such as diabetes, hypertension, as well as heart disease are commonly associated with obesity, which is typically a result of unhealthy lifestyle & poor dietary habits. Appropriately formulated weight reduction diet regimens can help, to some degree, manage the obesity epidemic. A very-low-carb and the high-fat ketogenic diet is one diet that has proven to be very successful for rapid weight loss. The ketogenic diet has special effects on the body and within the cells, providing benefits that go beyond what some other diet can offer. The mixture of carbohydrate restriction with ketone development decreases insulin levels, activates autophagy (cellular clean-up), improves efficiency and production of mitochondria, reduces inflammation as well as burns fat. A wide range of consequences offers a number of benefits with a number of different objectives and health issues for a number of different individuals. Overall, having high amounts of fat, moderate protein, as well as a low amount of carbohydrates can have a huge impact on your health-lowering your cholesterol, weight, blood sugar, & increasing your energy and mood levels.

In the beginning, a keto diet can be difficult to understand, but it's not as hard as it has been made to be. The change can be a bit hard, but clean eating's growing popularity makes it easier & easier to find low-carb foods available.

1.1 What is the ketogenic diet?

The term "ketogenic" is for a low-carb diet (such as the Atkins diet). The intention is for you to gain more calories from fat and protein, and lesser from carbohydrates. You cut most on easily digestible carbs, such as sugar, soda, pastries, and white bread.

A keto diet is a diet that is very low-carb; however, higher in fat. In many ways, this is similar to many other low-carb diets. Although you consume far fewer carbohydrates on the keto diet, keep moderate protein intake levels and could even increase your fat intake. Reducing carb intake puts the body in a metabolic state which is called ketosis, where fat is burned for energy from your food and from your body.

The "keto" in a ketogenic diet comes from the fact that it helps the body to produce tiny fuel molecules called "ketones." This is an additional source of fuel for the body, which is used when there is a lack of blood sugar (glucose). The liver creates ketones from fat when you consume very few carbs or hardly any calories. These ketones, therefore, serve as a source of fuel for the entire body, particularly for the brain. A brain is a hungry organ which consumes a lot of energy daily, and cannot run directly on fat. Only glucose-or ketones-can run it. On a ketogenic diet, all of the body changes its supply of fuel to work mostly on fat, burning fat 24-7.

The fat burning could increase dramatically when the insulin level becomes very low. To burn them off, it gets easier to reach your fat stores.

This is fantastic if you're trying to lose weight, but there may also be several fewer real benefits, such as less appetite and a stable supply of energy (we can get from high carb meals without the sugar peaks and valleys). This can help to keep you focused and alert.

This reaches a metabolic state which is called ketosis, whenever the body produces ketones. Fasting–not consuming anything–is the quickest way to get there, but no one can always fast forever. On the other side, a keto diet also contributes to ketosis and can be consumed continuously. It has many of the advantages of fasting without fasting long-term, including losing weight.

Basically, this is a diet that causes the body to discharge ketones into the bloodstream. Most cells tend to use carbohydrate-derived blood sugar as the principal source of energy for the body. Without blood sugar circulating from food, we begin to break apart stored fat into molecules named ketone bodies, the process is known as ketosis. When you hit ketosis, most cells can generate energy using ketone bodies before we begin to eat carbohydrates anymore. The change, from the use of circulating glucose to destroying stored fat as an energy source, usually occurs over 2 to 4 days of eating, fewer than 20 to 50 grams of carbs a day. Please note that this is a completely individual process, and to start producing sufficient ketones, some people have a much more restricted diet.

A ketogenic diet is high in fats and proteins, as it excludes carbohydrates. It usually includes lots of meats, processed meats, eggs, sausages, cheeses, nuts, butter, fish, oils, seeds, & fibrous vegetables.

It's really difficult to follow over the long run because it's so restrictive. Carbohydrates usually constitute at least 50% of the average US diet. One of the criticisms of keto diet is that several people, with very few vegetables and fruits, generally eat too much protein & poor-quality fats from packaged foods. Kidney disease patients need to be careful, as this diet may make their condition worse. In addition, some patients may initially feel a little tired, while others may experience bad breath, vomiting, nausea, constipation, and sleep disorders.

Biochemistry and Physiology:

Carbohydrates are essentially the main source of energy creation in body tissues. When the body is depleted of carbohydrates because the intake is reduced to less than 50g per day, the secretion of insulin is reduced significantly, and the body reaches a catabolic state. Glycogen stores are depleting, forcing the body to undergo certain metabolic alterations. When the supply of carbohydrates in body tissues is small, two metabolic processes take effect: gluconeogenesis & ketogenesis. Gluconeogenesis is the natural synthesis of glucose in the body, mainly from lactic acid, glycerol, and the amino acids alanine as well as glutamine in the liver. When the supply of glucose decreases more, the endogenous development of glucose cannot keep up with the body's needs, and ketogenesis starts to provide an alternative energy source in the form of ketone bodies.

Ketone bodies are replacements for glucose as the primary energy source. The stimulus for secretion of insulin is also low during ketogenesis due to the low blood glucose input, which greatly decreases the stimulus for fat & glucose storage. Certain hormonal changes can lead to the enhanced breakdown of fats causing fatty acids to grow. The fatty acids get metabolized into acetoacetate that is then converted into beta-hydroxybutyrate & acetone. These are the fundamental ketone bodies that aggregate in the body as maintained by a ketogenic diet. This metabolic state is attributed to "nutritional ketosis." Metabolism persists in ketoic conditions as long as the body is depleted of carbohydrates. The nutritional ketosis state is assumed very healthy, as ketone bodies are formed in small concentrations without altering blood pH. It differs greatly from ketoacidosis, a life-threatening disorder in which ketone bodies are developed in extremely large quantities, altering blood pH to an acidic state.

The synthesized ketone bodies in the body could be easily used by skin, muscle tissue, and kidneys for energy production. Ketone bodies can also cross the blood-brain wall to provide the brain with an alternate source of energy. Because of lack of mitochondria as well as enzyme diaphorase, RBCs and the liver don't use ketones either.

The development of the ketone body depends on many factors, including resting basal metabolic rate (BMR) and body mass index (BMI) and the percentage of body fat.

Ketone bodies create more adenosine triphosphate than glucose, often aptly referred to as "super fuel." One hundred grams of acetoacetate produce 9,400 grams of ATP, and 100g of beta-hydroxybutyrate produces 10,500 grams of ATP, while 100 grams of glucose yields just 8,700 grams of ATP. This helps the body even during a calorie deficit to sustain efficient fuel output. Ketone bodies also minimize free radical damage, thus increasing the antioxidant efficiency.

1.2 Overview of ketosis?

Ketosis is metabolic condition in which the body uses fat & ketones as its main source of fuel instead of glucose (sugar).

Glucose is contained in your liver & released for energy, as needed. However, those glucose stores become depleted after carbohydrate intake has been incredibly low for one to two days. Your liver may make certain glucose from an amino acid in the protein you eat through a process called gluconeogenesis but not quite enough to satisfy your brain's needs, which demands a constant supply of fuel. Luckily ketosis may provide an alternative energy source for you.

In ketosis, ketones are formed at an accelerated rate by your body.

Ketone bodies or ketones, are made from the fat you eat as well as your own body fat by your liver. Beta-hydroxybutyrate (BHB), acetoacetate, and acetone (though acetone is theoretically a breakdown acetate product) are the three ketone bodies.

Even though eating a higher-carb diet, the liver actually creates ketones on a regular base. This mostly happens overnight while you're sleeping but usually only in small amounts. But, as glucose and insulin levels go down on a carb-restricted diet, the liver speeds up its ketone production to provide your brain with energy.

Once the level of ketones hits a certain amount, you are found to have been in nutritional ketosis. The requirement for nutritional ketosis is at least 0.5 mmol/L of BHB (the ketone body contained in the blood), as per leading ketogenic diet experts Dr. Steve Phinney and Dr. Jeff Volek. Even though both fastings, as well as a keto diet, would allow you to get ketosis, just a keto diet is durable over long periods of time. In reality, it seems to be a safe way of eating that people can follow continuously.

Does the brain need carbohydrates?

There is a widespread yet mistaken belief that carbs are important for the proper functioning of the brain. In fact, if you ask any dietitians that how many carbs you should consume, they'll probably answer you need at least 130 grams per day to guarantee that your brain does have a constant supply of glucose. Yet that's not the case. In fact, even if you eat no carbs at all, your brain will stay healthy & functional. Although it is accurate that your brain gets high energy demands and needs some glucose, there are several ketones to provide a good portion of its energy when you're in ketosis. Luckily, your liver will always make up a limited amount of glucose needed by your brain, even under situations of complete hunger.

This mechanism, known as gluconeogenesis (absolutely "creating new glucose"), could also provide glucose to other organs that need it, like that of the red blood cells as well as a portion of the kidneys. This system has allowed our hunter-gatherer predecessors to go without eating for long periods because they always had accessibility to a fuel source: stored body fat. In fact, being in ketosis has no side effects on the functioning of the brain. On the other hand, many people have claimed that when they are in ketosis, they feel stronger mentally.

Nutritional ketosis vs. ketoacidosis

Nutritional ketosis & diabetic ketoacidosis are conditions which are completely different. Although nutritional ketosis is safe and health-beneficial, ketoacidosis is a medical emergency. Unfortunately, many medical professionals don't quite understand the difference between these two.

Ketoacidosis happens mainly in persons with type 1 diabetes if they don't take insulin. Blood sugar & ketones increase to dangerous levels in diabetic ketoacidosis (DKA), which interferes with the delicate acid-base balancing of the blood. People with ketoacidosis feel terribly ill and experience deep dehydration, vomiting, pain in the abdomen as well as weakness. DKA needs hospitalization, so IV fluids and insulin could be administered to gradually as well as safely lower blood sugar. BHB levels usually remain below 5 mmol/L in nutritional ketosis. People with diabetic ketoacidosis, however, often have BHB levels of 10 mmol/L or higher, which are directly linked to their failure to produce insulin.

When the blood ketone levels increase above a certain level, the insulin-capable pancreas can release enough yet to shut down anymore ketone production. In comparison, a patient with type 1 diabetes cannot produce insulin. And ketones can continue to rise to life-threatening rates unless insulin is provided by injection or IV.

Many people who may possibly become ketoacidosis are those who have type 2 diabetes who undergo medications known as SGLT2 inhibitors such as Invokana, Farxiga, or Jardiance. Sometimes, in rare cases, women who have no diabetes may develop ketoacidosis when breastfeeding. But, for most people who can produce insulin, ketoacidosis is almost unlikely.

Benefits of Ketosis:

Including providing a viable source of energy, ketones–and especially BHB –can help to lower inflammation as well as oxidative stress, which is claimed to play a part in the development of several chronic diseases. Indeed, in nutritional ketosis, there are several proven benefits as well as potential benefits.

Established benefits:

1. Appetite regulation: When they are in ketosis, one of the first things that people sometimes note is that they are no hungrier all the time. Studies have shown that to be in ketosis actually suppresses appetite. One study examined people who lost weight following an eight-week ketogenic diet and instead reintroduced minor amounts of carbs.

The researchers found that in those who stayed in ketosis, ghrelin levels (the "hunger hormone") were reduced, while those who weren't anymore longer in ketosis reported higher ghrelin levels.

2. Weight loss: If people limit carbohydrates, they automatically eat less and are given as much protein and fat as they require to feel full. Since ketogenic diets reduce appetite, lower insulin levels, as well as increasing fat burning, it's not shocking that other diets designed for weight loss have also been shown to outperform.

3. Reversal of diabetes & prediabetes: To be in ketosis may help stabilize blood sugar and insulin reaction in patients having type 2 diabetes or prediabetes, leading to a discontinuation of diabetes medication.

4. Potentially improved athletic performance: Ketosis can provide an extremely long-lasting supply of fuel for both high-level & recreational athletes during continuous exercise. 5. Seizure management: Trying to maintain ketosis with a conventional ketogenic diet or a less restrictive modified diet of Atkins (MAD) has been shown to be effective in managing epilepsy in adults and children who do not react to anti-seizure medication. Exciting early research also indicates that ketosis may be helpful for several other conditions, including reducing the frequency and intensity of anti-seizure medication. While work of superior quality is needed to validate these results, much of early studies are very promising.

Tips to get into ketosis

There are several ways you can safely and effectively get into nutritional ketosis.

1. Decrease daily net carbohydrate intake to less than 20 grams: Eating less than 20 grams of net carbs daily virtually guarantees that you will reach nutritional ketosis, although it is likely that you might not need to be this strict. What about 20 grams of carb?

2. Consider intermittent fasting: Going without food for 16-18 hours will help you get into ketosis faster. Simply skip breakfast or dinner, which can feel very normal on an appetite-suppressing keto diet, makes this easy to do.

3. Don't be afraid of fat: consuming plenty of fat is a good part of ketogenic eating! Ensure a source of healthy fat is included at each meal.

4. Cook with coconut oil: Besides being a natural fat that remains stable at high heat, coconut oil incorporates medium-chain fatty acids that might improve the production of ketone and may have other benefits as well.

5. Workout, if possible: You might not have enough energy to participate in intense physical activity throughout the shift to ketosis. Basically, going for only a brisk walk can, however, help you get more quickly into ketosis.

Ketosis happens when the body starts consuming energy from stored fat rather than glucose. Many studies have shown the powerful effects of a low carb diet, or keto, on weight loss. This diet could be hard to maintain, though, and can cause health problems in persons with these kinds of conditions, like type 1 diabetes.

DKA is an especially dangerous ketosis complication, which can happen when ketosis gets the blood very acidic. Emergency medication for people suffering from DKA is necessary. Many people can safely carry out the keto diet. Nonetheless, it is best to talk to a dietitian or doctor about any major changes to the diet. This is particular case for those with conditions underlying it.

1.3 Importance of Ketogenic Diet

A keto diet is basically an eating plan focusing on meals that provide plenty of healthy fats, adequate-protein, and so few carbohydrates. The aim is to gain more calories from the fat than from the carbohydrates. The diet functions by sapping the body of its stores of sugar. As a consequence, fat for energy will begin to break down. This results in the development of molecules named ketones, which the body needs for fuel. This may also cause weight loss when the body consumes fats.

As ketosis begins to break down fat reserves in the body, some keto diets strive to establish this metabolic state to encourage weight loss. Keto diets typically have high-fat content. For instance, 20 percent of the calories can be protein, 10 percent can be carbohydrates, and 70 percent can be fat. There are various versions, though. The proportions of the nutrients will depend on a person's version of the diet. Strict adherence to the keto diet may cause weight loss in the short term. This is partly due to people generally being able to ingest fewer calories before feeling hungry.

A ketogenic diet is healthy or not?

We have strong evidence that a ketogenic diet decreases children's seizure, sometimes just as effective as a medicine. Because of all these neuroprotective effects, for other neurological disorders such as Parkinson's, Alzheimer's, multiple sclerosis, autism, sleep disorders, and even brain cancer, questions regarding possible benefits have been raised. There have been no human statistics to support prescribing ketosis for the treatment of these conditions, however. The main reason, the patients are using the ketogenic diet is weight loss.

Prior research shows strong evidence of a quicker weight loss when the patients follow a ketogenic or very low carb diet relative to people on a more conventional low-fat diet, or maybe even a Mediterranean diet. But, over time, the gap in weight loss might seem to disappear. A ketogenic diet has also been shown to enhance blood sugar control, at least temporarily, in people with type 2 diabetes.

If we look at the impact on cholesterol levels, there's even more debate. Some studies show certain patients, in the beginning, have a rise in cholesterol levels, just to see cholesterol drop a few months later. But there is no long-term study that analyzes the impact on diabetes & high cholesterol over time.

A ketogenic diet may be an interesting alternative for treating other conditions and may result in weight loss acceleration. But it is difficult to follow, and this can be strong on red meat as well as other highly unhealthy, fatty, fried, and oily products.

We also don't know enough about its longer-term effects, possibly because it's so difficult to stick with that for a long-time people can't eat that way. It is also worth noting that "yo-yo diets" are linked to increased mortality, which leads to rapid loss of weight fluctuation. Instead of participating in the next trendy diet that would only last a few weeks to months (for most people, including a ketogenic diet), learn to embrace long-term sustainable change. A healthy, balanced diet, rich in very vibrant vegetables and fruits, lean meats, fish, whole grains, seeds, nuts, olive oil, and plenty of water does have the strongest evidence for a longer, healthier and vibrant existence.

1.4 How the adoption of a ketogenic diet is beneficial?

The ketogenic diet is surrounded by a lot of hype. Some experts claim that for most people, it's the best diet to follow, while others assume that's just another fad diet. Both sides of this debate are right, to some extent. There's not one perfect and proper diet for everybody or any condition, no matter how much people "believe" in it. The ketogenic diet poses no exception to this law.

The ketogenic diet, however, also has much strong research to support its advantages. In reality, it has been seen to be better than most of the diets helping people with:

- Epilepsy
- Type 2 Diabetes
- Type 1 Diabetes
- High Blood Pressure

- Alzheimer's disease

- Parkinson's disease

- Chronic Inflammation

- High Blood Sugar Levels

- Obesity

- Cardiac disease

- Polycystic Ovary Syndrome

- Fatty Liver Disease

- Cancer

- Migraines

However, if you are not a threat from any of these disorders, you may also consider the ketogenic diet beneficial. Some of the advantages most people have experienced are better functioning of the brain. Lower inflammation. A boost in energy. Enhanced body composition. The keto diet is having a wide range of benefits, is it really any beneficial than other diets?

Benefits of Keto diet:

1. Supports losing weight

The ketogenic diet can help to encourage weight loss in many ways, including metabolism enhancement and appetite reduction.

Ketogenic diets are foods that fill a person up and can even reduce the hormones that stimulate hunger.

For such reasons, a keto diet can lower the appetite as well as support weight loss. Researchers found that, in a 2013 meta-analysis of 13 separate randomized controlled trials, people who follow ketogenic diets decreased 2 pounds (lbs) more than all those following low-fat diets over 1 year. Likewise, another analysis of 11 studies showed that, after 6 months, people on a ketogenic diet dropped 5 pounds more than those on low-fat diets.

2. Helps improve acne

Acne has various causes, and in some people, it might have connections to diet & blood sugar. Having a diet high in processed & refined carbohydrates may change the balance of gut bacteria and lead to a significant increase and fall in blood sugar, both of which can negatively affect skin health. As per a 2012 study, a ketogenic diet may reduce acne ailments in some individuals by decreasing carb intake.

3. Might reduce the risk of some cancers

Researchers also explored the ketogenic diet's role in helping avoid or even cure other cancers. One study showed that the ketogenic diet could be a safe and appropriate alternative treatment for use in people with certain cancers, alongside chemo and radiation therapy. This is because, in cancer cells, it would trigger more oxidative stress than normal cells, letting them die.

A more recent 2018 study suggests that since the ketogenic diet lessens blood sugar, the risk of insulin abnormalities could also be lowered. Insulin is a blood sugar control hormone that can have ties to certain cancers.

Though some studies show the ketogenic diet might have some advantages in treating cancer, studies in such areas are limited. To better understand the real advantages of the ketogenic diet in cancer treatment and prevention, researchers need to perform further studies.

4. Can strengthen heart health

It is essential that when a person is following the ketogenic diet, he chooses healthy foods. Eating healthy, healthy fats, like avocados rather than less healthy fats, eg, pork rinds may help improve cardiovascular health by lowering cholesterol; some evidence suggests. A 2017 analysis of animal and human research on a keto diet found that some individuals experienced a significant decrease in total cholesterol levels, low-density lipoprotein (LDL), bad cholesterol, and triglycerides, as well as a rise in high-density lipoprotein (HDL), or "healthy" cholesterol. High cholesterol levels can increase the probability of developing heart disease. Consequently, reducing the impact of a keto diet on cholesterol will reduce the risk of heart problems in a person. The analysis concluded, however, that the positive effects of a diet on cardiovascular health depend on the quality of the diet. Hence eating healthy, nutritious food is important when following the keto diet.

5. Can protect the functionality of brain

Several types of research, such as this review in 2019, indicate the ketones produced during the keto diet have neuroprotective advantages, which means they can reinforce and defend the brain & nerve cells.

That is why a keto diet can help a person prohibit or handle conditions like Alzheimer's disease. Further work is, however, required into the effects of a keto diet on the brain.

6. Potentially lowers seizures

In a keto diet, the combination of fat, protein, and carbs changes the way the energy is used by the body, resulting in ketosis.

Ketosis is indeed a metabolic process in which ketone bodies are used by the body for food.

The Epilepsy Foundation indicates that ketosis, in people with epilepsy, can minimize seizures— particularly someone who has not responded to other various methods of treatment. More research needs to be done on how successful this is, although it tends to have far more impact on children with focal seizures. An analysis for 2019 supports the theory that a keto diet will benefit people with epilepsy. The ketogenic diet can reduce symptoms of epilepsy by multiple different processes.

7. Reduces PCOS illnesses

Polycystic ovarian syndrome (PCOS) is a hormonal condition that can contribute to excessive male hormones, ovulatory dysfunction, and ovaries. A high carbohydrate diet may cause adverse effects, such as skin issues and weight gain, in people with PCOS.

Clinical research on ketogenic diet & PCOS isn't enough. One 2005 pilot study evaluated five women for 24 weeks. The study found many PCOS markers improved with a ketogenic diet, including:

• Weight loss.

• Hormone balance.

• Luteinizing hormone (LH) ratios and follicle-stimulating hormone (FSH) ratios

• Rates of fasting insulin.

Another 2019 research review found a keto diet has positive effects for people having hormonal disorders, including PCOS with type 2 diabetes. They also made caution, however, that the findings were too complex to suggest a keto diet as a basic PCOS treatment.

Risks & complications

The ketogenic diet can offer a variety of health benefits. However, remaining on the long-term ketogenic diet can have an adverse health effect, including a higher risk of the below, mentioned health problems:

• Kidney stones.

• Large quantities protein in the blood.

• Deficiencies in minerals and vitamins;

• Fat build up in the liver.

The keto diet may cause harmful side effects known to many as keto flu. Such side effects could include

• Constipation.

• Fatigued.

• Low blood sugar.

• Nausea.

• Vomit.

- Headaches.

- Poor workout tolerance;

These symptoms are particularly common at the start of the diet, as the body adapts its new source of energy. Some people should eliminate the keto diet, including:

- Insulin-dependent people with diabetes.

- Those with eating disorders.

- Those with pancreatitis or kidney disease;

- Pregnant and breastfeeding mothers.

People who are taking a type of medication named sodium-glucose cotransporter 2 (SGLT2) inhibitors for type 2 diabetes must also not follow a keto diet. This treatment increases the chance of diabetic ketoacidosis, which is a dangerous condition that increases blood acidity.

Takeaway

It is important to talk to a doctor, dietitian, or trustworthy healthcare professional about any planned diet plan, particularly for people who try to control a health problem or disease. People who are looking to follow the keto diet should receive a doctor's consultation to test if they have diabetes, heart disease, hypoglycemia, or any other medical conditions to ensure a safe eating pattern for the keto diet. Note in mind that there is a lack of research on the long-term benefits of the ketogenic diet. It is uncertain whether it is more important to sustain the diet for longer periods than the less restrictive healthy eating habits.

A keto diet restricts carbohydrates or severely limits them. Some carbs do offer health benefits, however. People should eat a diet that includes a range of nutrient-dense, fibrous carbohydrates, such as vegetables and fruits, alongside balanced protein sources and healthy fats for a less strict dietary approach.

We've spent most of this chapter discussing how the keto diet helps people with various conditions, but there are a few benefits that anyone can get. Below are four major benefits of a ketogenic diet.

1. Boosts functioning of the brain

Brain cells become more efficient after consumption of a ketogenic diet, brain inflammation decreases, as well as neurotrophic factors that promote health, are activated.

This is triggered by the mixture of restriction of carbohydrates with the use of ketone. In particular, ketones give the brain a chance to regulate the neurotransmitters named Glutamate & GABA (gamma-Aminobutyric acid). Glutamate is the body's primary excitation neurotransmitter (promoting stimulation), and GABA is the body's principle inhibitory neurotransmitter (reduces stimulation).

Brain fog and lack of focus may be associated with having too little GABA and too much Glutamate. This will occur if your brain needs to use power with Glutamate & glutamic acid, which leaves nothing left to be converted into GABA. By providing the brain some other form of energy when breaking down ketones, you can balance out the development of neurotransmitters.

This balance (rise in the production of GABA) helps to reduce excess neuronal firing in the brain, resulting in a better mental focus. An additional benefit of more GABA development is a reduction in anxiety and stress and a greater sense of calm.

2. Improves Energy

Research has shown that those who adopt a ketogenic diet build better mitochondrial function and generate fewer reactive oxygen species, as mentioned earlier. Good mitochondrial function for your cells equates to more energy while getting less reactive oxygen species to enhance energy efficiency. In other words, the keto diet allows you to make the most of your cells so you could get the more out of your life.

3. Decreases Pain and Inflammation

Without the additional damage caused by oxidative stress, the body's inflammatory pathways need not be used as often to repair the damage.

That reduces levels of inflammation in the body. A good side effect of the anti-inflammatory advantages of these is that chronic pain patients may also experience a reduction in pain.

4. Enhances Body Composition

Most studies suggest that when it comes to losing weight, a ketogenic diet is superior to caloric intake. For example, one study divided 132 participants into 2 groups: a low-carb diet (30g or less of carbs a day) group, and a low-fat diet group with restricted calories.

Following six months of this dietary experiment, the researchers found that "severely obese participants with a higher prevalence of diabetes & metabolic syndrome lost a lot of weight on a carbohydrate-restricted diet in a six-month period than on fat and calorie-restricted diet." When you limit carbohydrates, then the extra pounds may decrease. This is great for people wanting to lose weight, and what about people wanting to gain muscle? The keto diet is beneficial for muscle mass growth. That's because you'll eat a lot more protein than a lot of other diets.

Chapter 2: Types of Ketogenic Diet

A ketogenic diet is one that is designed to cause ketosis, to break down body fat in ketones, and to allow the body to operate primarily on ketones instead of glucose. There have been several ways to bring about ketosis, and hence there are a variety of different forms of a ketogenic diet.

Even though the end goal of such diets is the same, the various types of ketogenic diets typically share a lot of similarities, particularly low in carbohydrates and high in dietary fat. Luckily, a few keto variants have been produced, which are much more stable and more comfortable to adhere to in the long run. The conventional or regular ketogenic diet brings the body into ketosis: you use fat (instead of carbs) as your primary source of fuel in this metabolic state, which encourages the loss of weight. The body will go into an out of ketosis on a changed keto diet but still, lose weight & body fat.

There's no best diet that suits everyone, not the keto diet even. Even if you're an ingrained carbophobe or a beginner to the keto lifestyle, the only way of learning much about what fits you and what isn't is to try new dietary strategies. Do not be afraid to work with each keto diet modification and then see how these make you feel if you choose to adopt the keto diet. There is nothing to lose but everything to gain for you, so what do you wait for? Make this happen!

2.1 Standard Ketogenic Diet (SKD)

If you're trying for weight loss or you're living a rather sedentary lifestyle, therefore the standard ketogenic diet is a good starting point. This is the "real" keto diet, as you won't eat a lot of carbs at all, usually 30 g or less a day.

There are several alterations to the ketogenic diet. Most individuals adopt the standard ketogenic diet program, which offers about 10% of your total calories from carbs. Yet generally, if you intend on taking a ketogenic diet, you will target at eating fewer than 10% of your overall calories from carbs per day. The majority of the calories remaining should be 20-30% protein and 60-80% fat. That implies no more than 200 calories (or 50 grams) may come from carbs if you adopt a regular 2,000-calorie diet, whereas 400 to 600 calories may come from protein as well as 1,200 to 1,600 may come from fat. (There's a reason this program is also called a low-carb, high-fat diet!)

Is workout required in Standard Ketogenic Diet?

Even though the keto diet does not especially require exercise to be implemented into your lifestyle, it is always necessary to increase physical activity in order to help reduce and maintain a healthy weight. Among endurance athletes, the switch to a ketogenic diet can minimize post-training recovery time, but for casual workouts, the transfer to a ketogenic diet can initially make sticking to your workout routine a challenge. If you find your energy levels falling too much when you start your ketogenic diet, decelerate your carbohydrate reduction and make sure you do it over time, rather than at once.

Expected Side Effects:

Start changing your meal plan slowly to avoid side effects such as keto flu. Start by knowing how many carbs you will be taking in most days. Then start reducing your carb intake progressively over a period of some weeks, while increasing your dietary fat intake steadily to maintain your calorie the same. Additionally, you will seek assistance from a professional to ensure that this strategy works best for both you and your health goals. "See a dietitian & adapt the diet to match your long-term requirements," Spano suggests.

What to eat

The keto diet is not a formal meal plan, so following this diet does not entail any costs or dues. But that eating approach can maximize your food bill based on your present food habits.

Since many processed foods will not be found ketogenic-friendly, at the time, a move to buying many wholes, unprocessed foods might seem costly, particularly with high-fat & protein-rich foods in mind. Yet buying fresh produce, in-season, along with frozen veg, which can be as safe as their fresh equivalents, will help cut costs. While nuts, seeds, & animal proteins like beef can increase the cost of the food bill, bulk buying may also help to lower the cost.

The keto diet is highly dependent on dietary fat. Since high animal fat levels in the diet are associated with increased cholesterol levels, it may be beneficial to include a great variety of plant-based fats. Plant oils like olive oil & avocado oil have healthy cooking fat & dressings.

Including fat-rich foods like avocado, nuts, as well as seeds can all create healthy options to provide unsaturated fats and together with helpful fiber. Some fruits on this menu are limited— there are cases, like avocado— but non-starchy vegetables, including leafy greens, might become a part of your diet. This diet can also include lean proteins like fish poultry, as well as grass-fed beef as a protein source.

A-List of suitable Standard Keto Diet Foods

• Non-starchy vegetables, such as leafy greens, cauliflower, cauliflower, chili peppers, mushroom, and onions.

• Dairy, like cheese and eggs.

• Proteins such as beef, pork, chicken, fish, shellfish, & soya.

Almonds, nuts, pistachios, sunflower seeds, and pumpkin seeds.

• Fats, such as plant oils & butter.

• Fruit such as avocado, berries, and coconut (in moderation), and rhubarb.

Foods You have to Avoid or Restrict on the Keto diet

• Processed foods such as crackers, chips of corn, and chips of potato.

• Sweets, including desserts, pies, brownies, and cookies.

• All kinds of grains, like bread and pasta, rice, and quinoa.

• High-carb crops, like tropical fruits and melons.

• Artificial sweeteners like Equal & Splenda.

A Regular Ketogenic Diet Sample 3-Day Menu

Day 1

- Breakfast: Sliced avocado scrambled eggs.

- Snack: On celery, have almond butter.

- Lunch: spinach salad with canned tuna, vinegar, and olive oil.

- Snack: 1 oz string cheese plus 1 oz pistachios.

- Dinner: steak sirloin served alongside sautéed mushroom, onions, and rice with cauliflower.

Day 2

- Breakfast: Sliced bacon with mushroom & cheese omelet.

- Snack: half avocado.

- Lunch: Stir-fry the chicken with peppers, onions & peanuts sautéed by peanut oil.

- Snack: 1 oz Brie cheese along with 1 oz walnuts.

- Dinner: Salmon fillet along with oven-roasted Brussels sprouts.

Day 3

- Breakfast: keto shake made with avocado, chia seeds, full-fat coconut milk & nut butter.

- Snack: Tough-boiled egg.

- Lunch: Cheeseburger over a bed of lettuce served with string beans (without bun).

- Snack: 1 ounce's almonds.

- Dinner: Chicken breast with broccoli (sautéed).

2.2 Targeted Keto Diet (TKD)

Simply put, the Targeted Ketogenic Diet (TKD) is nothing more than a normal keto diet–except eating carbs during your workout time. Which ensures you can eat carbohydrates every day you work out. If your target is still a fat loss, try to ensure that your calorie total amount for that day contains the additional calories from the carbohydrates. It suggests that these days fewer fats should be eaten.

The TKD is intended for persons who exercise at high intensities on a regular basis or for longer time periods. On the other side, if you're sedentary or merely exercise at low intensity a few times in a week, then maybe the standard keto diet is all you require.

What to eat?

Many people who experiment with TKD note that 25-50 g of carbohydrate taken 30 minutes before exercise is the best performance for them.

Most suggest eating plain, easily digestible carbohydrates, including liquids or highly glycemic foods that dissolve quickly into the body — sweets, white bread, and candy bars. Yet dextrose and glucose would be the perfect sources of carbohydrates for a good TKD.

You would like to avoid fructose because it appears to go straight to the liver to refill glycogen in the liver (rather than heading to the muscle we want). The foods with the highest fructose happen to be natural foods such as berries and honey. On the other hand, stuff like gummy bears, candies, Gatorade, & Powerade is some decent carb sources for TKD.

Individuals have also shown excellent results in taking natural maple syrup before workouts. All those options, however, still contain a good amount of fructose. Consider supplementing it with dextrose tablets or packets of glucose gel to get the pure form of glucose. These will give you a pure form of glucose with no fructose, allowing them the TKD's cleanest carb sources. Whatever carb source you want, it must be consumed either alone or with proteins (for a muscle-building effect). In general, fat intake should be prevented directly from pre- and post-exercise. Dietary fat tends to slow protein and carbohydrate digestion, which is something you don't want when implementing the TKD. Only fats that will not affect the digestion of carb or protein are medium-chain triglycerides (MCTs) since they are digested faster than any other fat. These also help improve the ketone levels as a side benefit, if you consume carbs or not. If you're looking to enhance your ketone levels, this allows MCTs a fine addition to your before or after the workout meal.

The Takeaway: Have 25-50 grams of carbohydrates from high-glucose, non-fat products such as hard candies, gummy bears, Gatorade, Powerade as well as pure maple syrup. Cleaner sources of glucose, such as dextrose supplements and packs of glucose gel, can be even more powerful. They are using protein with carbs to improve muscle growth and/or MCTs to raise ketone levels.

Benefits of Targeted Ketogenic Diet:

The TKD is a "balance" between a Standard Ketogenic Diet & a Cyclical Ketogenic Diet, ensuring you can still do high-intensity exercise, but for long periods of time, you won't have to be out of ketosis.

TKD will help you endure performance throughout the high-intensity exercise for most people's purposes-though not as much as CKD. To intermediate or beginner strength athletes, or those who are unable to use a CKD diet for health reasons, it is most suitable. So far, there is no study that show weight training drawbacks based on low blood glucose sources. There have been studies that offer carbs before resistance & strength training, but in the long run, they have not found any higher performance. However, when they eat pre-workout carbohydrates, many SKD keto-ers record strength & endurance enhancements during high-intensity activities. This is largely because of the fact that most forms of anaerobic training need glucose for the muscles to fuel. By adopting the targeted keto diet, when you offer the muscles the glucose they need, they will react with the ability to conduct at high intensities for prolonged periods of time.

When these same muscles do not have enough glucose, they're going to lack stamina and strength during activities that constantly require a significant effort for 15-300 sec. Endurance athletes and exercisers of moderate-intensity may also benefit from the targeted keto diet while engaging in activities that last an hour or a half or longer.

Studies have found that supplementing by carbohydrates before performing long endurance tasks such as running a half marathon may enhance performance and the runners ' perceived exertion without affecting ketosis.

Not clear what They mean by a lowering of perceived exertion? Here is one example. Before exercising, if you eat 25-50 grams of carbs and you find that this task is easier to achieve similar to doing the same exercise without the extra carbs, this means that your perceived exertion has decreased. Although this has only occurred during a half-marathon in research on endurance runners, this effect may also describe why many keto'ers report having improved endurance and strength during high-intensity exercise.

When working out, another advantage of eating carbs is the impact it has on levels of insulin. Yeah, high levels of insulin are the complete opposite of what you'd like to have with the keto diet, but insulin rises can be helpful at the right times. Increasing levels of insulin prior to exercise, for example, does have an anabolic effect on muscles, avoiding muscle breakdown, also promoting muscle development. Although using the TKD, you may experience a performance improvement and a perfectly executed insulin response; these aren't the primary objectives of this dietary plan. The primary reason behind that is to retain glycogen levels; then, you're basically setting up for another workout.

The Takeaway: To summarize this section clearly, if you are an athlete or if you're doing routine workouts and your progress has been declining, then I suggest that you test with carbohydrates before practicing.

By doing so, you may help retain your glycogen stores, reduce the exercise's hardness, and increase strength and endurance.

Will Targeted Keto Diet Kick me out of Ketosis?

With the excess of carbohydrates, you take in before exercise, the rates of your ketones will eventually decrease. By how much more are they going to drop? It depends on that. Most will find that, due to the greater levels of insulin, they drop out of ketosis for a few hours after their exercise.

The great news is that you will be carrying out different systemic changes that will help you move back into ketosis. Exercising, for example, will help to increase insulin sensitivity, meaning less insulin would be required to handle the 25-50 grams you consume on the TKD. As a result of the exercise, the cell membrane protein named glucose transporters will also become more active, transforming the muscles into a glucose trap that sucks up blood sugar.

The mixture of increased insulin sensitivity with glucose transporter activity will mean that the carbohydrates will be used up by muscle, insulin levels will drop, and the production of ketone will be speeded up sooner rather than later. If you want to naturally raise your ketone levels, you could do some low-intensity exercise to help lower your insulin even further and increase your blood's free fatty acids (further free fatty acids= further ketones). Another technique you can use to raise ketone rates is to supplement your workout with MCTs prior, during, or after.

Irrespective of your insulin & blood sugar levels, these fatty acids would be transformed into ketones. However, it is important to remember that either of those ketone boosting methods may not need to be used. Your ketone levels rely on many factors such as your exercise intensity, duration of the workout, levels of stress, how keto-adapted are you, and insulin levels, although you may remain in ketosis after you have ingested the carbohydrates pre-workout. On the other side, you could stop the production of ketones for a few hours entirely. Does that really mean you should be observing your ketone rates rigidly before, during, & after your TKD workouts? Although you can test the ketones and figure out whether or not you are in ketosis, this is absolutely unnecessary. The essential thing after your workout is that you adhere to your ketogenic diet schedule. If you do that, in a few hours, you'll be in ketosis, and your tests won't suffer at all. The Takeaway: Consuming pre-workout carbs will lower the ketone rates. How much the drop in your ketone levels depends on several factors, but as long as you adhere to the ketogenic diet, there's no problem in getting back into ketosis. If you want to raise your ketone levels, then after your workout, do some low-intensity exercise and/or supplement with MCTs.

How to use Targeted Ketogenic Diet?

Here's how you can do the TKD correctly and get the best outcomes:

- If you're on an SKD and want to do high-intensity workout, you'll have to eat carbohydrates during your exercise at some stage. The way you measure your macros is going to be exactly the same, except you have to take into consideration the additional calories you will get from eating carbohydrates–modify your fats as required. (More accurately, each gram of carb is equal to 4 calories, while each gram of fat is equal to 9 calories. If your objective is to losing weight, this implies you will decrease your fat intake by about 11 grams when you eat 25 grams of carbs on workdays.) The ideal time to eat carbs is 30-60 minutes before your exercise, where you should eat about 25-50 grams of carbohydrate. It's recommended that you eat high GI carbs that absorb quickly.

- Hard candies, sugary sports drinks, gummy bears, natural maple syrup/sugar and dextrose supplements, as well as glucose gels, are the best carb sources for the TKD.

- Stick to sources of a sugar high in glucose, since fructose may refill glycogen in the liver and disrupt ketosis.

- At this time, most fats must be avoided, because they slow down the process of digestion. If you need fat before the exercise, then you should have MCTs.

- If you need to ingest more than 50 g of carbs during your workout, then try splitting it up–take half of those carbs 30 mins prior to the workout as well as half right before you start.

- If you eat post-workout carbohydrates, then the limit is 25-50 g. (This technique will hold you out of ketosis for long periods of time) Instead of ingesting post-workout carbohydrates, have a strong-quality protein smoothie to enhance recovery. Post-workout carbohydrates are absolutely unnecessary.

- If you have different training practices a day, split your 25-50 g of carbs between the two sessions or change your carbohydrate intake according to duration and intensity (e.g.,15 g for the first session & 25 g for the second).

- Experiment with proven supplements to boost performance, including creatine, taurine, and beta-alanine, L-citrulline, and MCTs.

- If you don't follow the TKD, probably try out the cyclical keto diet.

2.3 Cyclical keto diet (CKD)

One of the main concepts of a keto diet is to reduce as much as feasible of the carbohydrates. Of this purpose, many athletes & bodybuilders reject low carb, high fat diet because they are afraid their performance will be hindered by it. Fortunately, there are many variations in the keto diet, which makes it perfect for just about everyone. A cyclical ketogenic diet is essentially a form of the keto diet that allows for some carb intake while still reaping the rewards of ketosis. We'll talk more about what the cyclical keto diet is, and how to adopt it.

What is the Cyclical Keto diet?

The cyclical keto diet (CKD) is a modification of the ketogenic diet, which includes consuming clean carbs, one or two days a week. A regular ketogenic diet comprising of very low carbs, moderate protein, with high fats should adopt the other five to six days.

You're advised to eat large quantities of carbs such as pasta, rice, beans, oatmeal, and whole grains during the 1 or 2 days of carbs— often defined as carb loading. But, to achieve the best outcomes, it's just as essential that you keep your intake of fat low during your carbohydrate days.

For a cyclical ketogenic diet, the normal format is 5-6 days of a ketogenic diet and 1-2 days of high carb consumption. Others also experimented with 2 weeks periods, where there are 10-12 days of ketogenic nature and 3-4 days of carb load. The break of 2 weeks has also had positive results, but it does not work as easily into everybody's schedules. The primary aim here is to temporarily turn off ketosis to replace glycogen muscle in order to improve efficiency in the next period of training. If for health issues (hyperinsulinemia or hypertension) you are on a ketogenic diet, you may discover the cyclical ketogenic diet unfeasible as the hormonal response will cause health symptoms that are handled with a low carb diet. The literature review on cyclical ketogenic diets is limited. However, there are two 2017 scientific studies that give us proof that a good idea for athletes is to combine the ketogenic diet with carb re-feeding.

In one study, for ten weeks, twenty-five men of college-age were divided into a keto diet group as well as a western diet group. The keto dietitians were set on the western diet for one week after the ten weeks. The findings are stunning. During the first ten weeks, there was not much distinction between two groups; but, after one week on a western diet, the keto diet group experienced a major improvement in average body mass as well as power output on the Wingate Power Test (cycling at peak intensity for a short time). There were no similar changes discovered in the western diet team.

What the Science Says About Cyclical Ketogenic Diets In another 2017 research, researchers studied the effects that a low carb diet, a high carb diet, as well as a periodized high carb diet (similar to a cyclical ketogenic diet) on elite race walkers. The results demonstrate many doubts that a strict low-carb diet may hurt performance at higher levels of intensity, but what did happen to race walkers on the high-carb diet that was periodic? They witnessed a defined performance improvement.

While these two types of research do not check the same cyclical ketogenic diet regimen we recommend in this article, they provide proof that you can combine the ketogenic diet with a high carbohydrate diet to boost athletic performance and body composition. You don't have to follow the diets used by these researchers to get those tests, though. All you need to do is adopt the cyclical ketogenic diet by depleting glycogen stores, going into ketosis, and then replenishing glycogen stores with one or two days of carb refeeding. You get the advantages of keto-adaptation, ketones, and carbohydrates this way.

Who Can Gain an advantage from the Cyclical Keto diet?

The primary reason for adopting a ketogenic diet is for health issues like epilepsy, hyperinsulinemia, or metabolic disease like type 2 diabetes; you are not recommended for the cyclical ketogenic diet. Furthermore, CKD can be avoided if you're a total beginner to diet or keto in general. The cyclical keto diet is regarded as an adaptive eating regimen aimed at people who lead an active lifestyle and are familiar with nutrition.

CKD is a perfect keto diet system for:

- People who frequently do exercise.

- Professional dietitians, with nutrition experience.

- Bodybuilders hoping to muscle building.

- Athletes trying to improve performance in their workouts.

The Objective of Carbs on Keto:

The aim of the cyclical keto diet is to quit ketosis temporarily to fill the muscle glycogen of your body, in order to improve your exercises or athletic output for the rest of the week. The body depends heavily on glucose (from carbs) instead of ketones (from fat) during high-intensity workouts. If you implement one or two carbohydrate days, your body rewards from several various processes that enable you to improve muscle and develop greater strength. Here's how it goes: 1. Anabolic hormones are getting increasing. Testosterone, IGF-1 (insulin-like growth factor 1), & growth hormones have all been responsible for enhancing your strength, physique, and performance. Following a CKD, you give your body the macronutrients it wants to balance these hormones.

2. Insulin is a must for athletes and bodybuilders

It happens because when you eat carbs, insulin gets increased. It will refill your glucose reserves as insulin is elevated in your carb days. Your muscles are, literally, like glycogen tanks. Extra muscle glycogen means you're going to have better exercise results, and the one or two carbohydrate days will allow you to keep those stores full for the rest of the week.

3. Standard Days of Ketogenic Diet Increases testosterone & Growth Hormone

The growth hormone blunts when the insulin becomes high. Yet even on your carb days, you are just raising insulin, your body will benefit from extra growth hormone increases if you eat low carb, macronutrient intake, and high fat on non-carb days. Additionally, high-fat intakes should complement your non-carbohydrate days. Studies have also shown that high-fat consumption improves total levels of testosterone.

How to Begin Cyclical Keto diet?

Now that you learn how athletes & bodybuilders can benefit from CKD let's give you a simple blueprint to get started. The aim is to re-enter ketosis after your carb days, as soon as possible. This means that your exercises should be hard, compound lifts after those carb-ups, which will help you rapidly deplete glucose & re-enter ketosis.

In your 1-2 carbohydrate days:

• Carbohydrates must make up 70% of total calorie consumption for the day.

• Protein will make up 15% of total calories.

• Fat accounts for 15% of total calories.

• Carbohydrates will include whole-grain, rice, lentils, potatoes, black beans, also pasta. (Try as far as possible to stop the refined carbs).

In the other 5-6 keto days:

• Fats must make up nearly 65% of your caloric intake.

• Protein will make up 15-25% of total calories.

• Fewer than 10% must come from carbs.

• Take your fats from nutritious sources, including avocados, eggs, fatty meats, and coconut oil.

What to Choose? Targeted Keto Diet or Cyclical Keto Diet?

The cyclical keto diet dedicates one to two Complete days of high carbohydrate intake to completely refill glycogen reserves in the muscles and liver. This implies that the cyclical ketogenic diet is just not for those who are unable to execute the required amount or strength of training.

For instance, for low to medium intensity trainers & exercise newcomers, this diet modification is not recommended as they are most likely unable to completely deplete their glycogen stores and return to ketosis if they adopt the cyclical keto diet. For that reason, a Targeted Keto diet is the perfect way for you to use carbs as a performance-enhancing tool, whether you are a beginner or intermediate athlete, or do ultra-endurance exercise. On the other side, if your strict routine of training requires high-intensity exercises that reduce your glycogen reserves, helping you to fall back into ketosis every week, then maybe the cyclical keto diet is for you. The primary aim of the cyclical keto diet is to use carbohydrates as a method to improve muscle growth & exercise efficiency, while the standard keto diet also benefits you. The downside, however, is that with the extra muscle mass, you may gain some body fat.

Putting it all together:

When you are on a standard keto diet and frequently do high-intensity exercise, then you can benefit much from a cyclical ketogenic diet. In this dietary method, you can combine the rewards of burning ketones with the availability of enough sugar to boost efficiency, strength & muscle gain.

The most popular method of the cyclical keto diet is 5-6 days of a standard keto diet with 1-2 days of high carbohydrate refeeding. Make sure you perform fasted high-intensity training during the cycle's ketogenic diet process to replenish your glycogen reserves, thus driving the body into ketosis faster. It is best to eat complex carbs from whole food sources during your carb refeed because high GI foods will hinder your ability to return to ketosis.

We suggest you get at least 70% of your calories from carb sources such as potatoes, carrots, yams, bananas, pineapples, and white rice on the first day.

It's better to reduce the carb consumption by 10% during the second day and consume lower GI carbs, including whole grains, blueberries, lentils, peas, and black beans. Keep on replenishing your glycogen while increasing your ketone levels again after your carb re-feed & repeat the process. That's it. Through following this nutritional plan, you will potentially reap the advantages of a high carb diet and a keto diet. Nonetheless, if you do not exercise regularly at high intensities or if you are a beginner of the exercise, either the standard keto diet or the targeted keto diet is the better choice for you.

2.4 High protein keto diet (HPKD)

This diet contains more protein than that of a standard ketogenic diet, with 35% protein, 60% fat and 5% carbs. Studies show a high protein keto diet is beneficial for weight loss in people who need to lose weight. Just like other types of a keto diet, there is indeed a lack of research into if there are any health hazards if followed for many years.

What is protein?

Protein consists of a few smaller components called amino acids. While your body could make much of the 20 amino acids it needs, there are nine which it cannot produce. They are defined as the essential amino acids, as they have to be eaten every day in food. Since animal foods possess all 9 essential amino acids in nearly the same amounts, they are called "complete" protein. In comparison, one or more essential amino acids are missing in plants and have been considered "incomplete" protein. Sources of keto-friendly animal protein contain meat, poultry, fish, eggs, & cheese. Keto-friendly sources of plant protein include most seeds and nuts, while some are greater in carbs than others.

What does protein do in the body?

Protein is an integral part of any cell in your body. It is split down into individual amino acids that are absorbed into the muscles as well as other tissues when you eat protein. There are only a few significant functions of the protein: repair and development of the muscle. The protein in the muscles is usually torn down and replaced on a regular basis, and a fresh supply of amino acids is required for the synthesis of muscle proteins, producing new muscle. Consuming enough dietary protein helps to avoid muscle loss and fosters muscle development when combined with resistance training — maintaining the internal organs, healthy skin, hair, nails & bones. Because the protein turnover occurs more gradually in these structures than those in the body, new amino acids are needed to replace the ones that become old and destroyed over time — hormone & enzyme formation. Many of the life-needed hormones-including insulin & growth hormone-are also proteins. In the human body, too, most enzymes are proteins. To make these essential substances, your body relies on a constant supply of amino acids. Additionally, having enough protein will help improve weight control. Protein, for example, has been used to minimize appetite and prevent overeating by activating hormones that encourage feelings of happiness & fulfillment. Your body also consumes more protein-digesting calories as a comparison with fat or carbohydrates.

Is Too Much Keto-Friendly Protein?

Consuming too much protein is among the main concerns for people who just start their keto diets.

However, the body generates ketones from fat so you can hold down to a minimum the protein and carbs, right? It is not necessary.

Carbohydrates are the macronutrient only that can actually interfere with ketosis, which is why watching for hidden carbs and finding the carbohydrate limit which suits you is important. In addition, eating protein does not affect your ketone levels. You should eat high-fat & high-protein (fatty cuts of grass-fed meat preferably) and remain in ketosis. This is why many persons who are transitioning from keto to carnivore diet face no problem remaining in nutritional ketosis.

So, what about Gluconeogenesis (GNG)?

GNG is a real & necessary process already occurring inside your body. It's not ketosis's enemy. It actually allows for ketosis in the first place.

The High-Protein Misconception: Don't Fear Gluconeogenesis.

There is a commonly circulated argument that excess protein is harmful to ketosis because Gluconeogenesis is caused by it. The theory has been disproved ever since. However, there are many published articles online citing this baseless assertion, so understanding how GNG operates on ketosis is important. Gluconeogenesis (GNG) is a metabolic process that enables the development of glucose from non-carb sources in your kidneys and liver.

The word Gluconeogenesis is divided into three parts: Gluco: came from the Greek root glukos–actually means "sweet wine." Neo: "new". Genesis: "creation". Thinking about GNG like: It's how the body makes new sweet wine for your body. This process is special in that it's producing glucose from anything other than carbohydrates.

Your body takes compounds such as lactate, amino acids (protein), & glycerol to produce glucose when there is no carbohydrate around.

When you try to operate on ketones instead of glucose, this may seem like a challenge, but the reality is that Gluconeogenesis has an extremely important function, it doesn't damage ketosis. Some people claim that to survive you don't need carbs which is only true to some extent. To clarify, you do not have to consume any high-carbohydrate foods to sustain, but don't make any mistake— your body requires glucose as well as glycogen to keep you healthy (as well as in ketosis), and this will be achieved through survival mechanisms such as Gluconeogenesis.

Why Is Gluconeogenesis Essential?

On a keto diet, Gluconeogenesis is used for three main purposes in the body.

Preventing hypoglycemia: Even in ketosis, the glucose levels will never go down to zero. GNG maintains a safe balance of the blood sugar, so it does not drop to harmful levels (aka hypoglycemia).

Fueling tissues that cannot use ketones: The body has a number of cells that can only use glucose for existing, like red blood cells, kidney medulla (inner part of your kidney), testicles, and certain parts of your brain. Ketones can accommodate up to 70% of the energy needs of your brain, while GNG glucose incorporates the rest. The other organs absolutely can't metabolize ketones. Hence, Gluconeogenesis gives them sufficient glucose to stay healthy.

Resupplying glycogen stores: You may replenish muscle glycogen via the GNG that occurs during ketosis— at least if you 're not really a pro athlete or participate in contests. During workouts, glycogen is essential to muscle recovery.

If GNG did not generate enough glucose to support these functions, your body would never be able to make the transition to use ketones for energy because certain cells (like RBC's) would die, and your blood sugar would fall too low.

Gluconeogenesis allows for a ketosis

Can Additional Protein Rise Glucose From GNG?

GNG represents an extremely stable mechanism. Also, with extra protein, it isn't easy to increase. Gluconeogenesis does not work at the same pace as carbohydrate metabolism (creating glucose from carbs). In response to the sugar, when you eat chocolate cake, your blood glucose rapidly goes up. When you eat extra fat, this will not raise your blood glucose the same way. Studies have shown that even with extra amino acids, GNG production doesn't increase.

The following points are obvious by now:

- Gluconeogenesis is the mechanism of producing internal glucose by non-carb sources, like protein.

- Survival requires Gluconeogenesis.
- Gluconeogenesis allows for ketosis.
- Eating too much protein will not enhance the gluconeogenesis rate.
- Yet protein eating isn't just safe; it's required.

3 Reasons That Why You Should Eat More Protein on Keto

Sufficient protein consumption is important in the ketogenic diet. It helps the body to be in a fat-burning state; it has fewer calories, and not eating enough protein is harmful.

#1: Protein Helps with Fat Loss

Many people on keto would reduce their protein to 30-40g, limit their total carbs to 10-20g, and only consume excess fat. It is a common error. Excessive protein intake is a perfect way to address your keto diet program if your aim is to lose fat. It's for these reasons:

1. Protein satiates more than fat.

2. Proteins are very dense in nutrients.

3. If protein is low, people are likely to over-eat.

Moreover, using your stored body fat for energy is the most efficient way to begin losing weight on keto, not the fresh dietary fat you're consuming. When you consume so much fat, your body will take in the fresh fat and will not have the opportunity to take your accumulated fat reserves. By increasing the protein and reducing the fat intake, you can conquer weight loss plateaus.

#2: Protein Provides Less Calories Than Fat.

For burning protein, the body has to use further energy (calories) than burning fat. For example, if you consume a 100-calorie grass-fed beef serving, your body could store only 75 percent of it as calories, as it needs 25 percent of calories to consume and then use it as fuel. Alternatively, you store up to 98 percent of it as calories if you eat fat. It means that you store almost all the calories from fat, while you can store less of protein when you get some of the calories to consume it.

#3: Insufficiency of protein is harmful.

Not having adequate protein on keto has severe side effects, including:

1. Worsened exercise performance: You won't be able to sustain muscle mass with little or no protein.

2. Neuron atrophy: Amino acids are needed in your brain to function properly. Research suggests a diet with a protein deficiency can contribute to atrophy and loss of neurons.

3.Weaker immune system: An amino acid arginine deficiency will lead to the malfunction of your T cells— cells that control your immunity.

4. Increased disease risk: A deficiency of amino acids could raise the risk of having certain illnesses, including sickle cell disease, cystic fibrosis, and pulmonary hypertension, acute asthma, cardiovascular disease, and some cancer.

Many of these keto adverse effects result from consuming too little protein:

- Thyroid problems.
- Plateaus to weight loss.

- Hormonal problems.
- Hair loss.

Now that we know why protein is required choosing the best possible sources of protein for your diet is important.

How much protein would you eat on Keto?

The Standard American Diet (SAD) is heavy in carbs, with certain protein but very little fat. On keto, with the majority of your calories originating from fat, few calories originating from protein, and very less from carbohydrates, you take a completely opposite approach. Although each person has different needs, most people are following these guidelines for macronutrients to enter (or stay in) ketosis: 75-80 percent of calories must come from fat. Protein will be responsible for 20 percent of calories. Carbohydrates will make up 5% of calories. That's a common way of breaking down your ketogenic diet macros. And although it may help you start generating ketones, the most powerful solution to general body structure and weight loss may not be that.

There is a better alternative, instead of setting macronutrient amounts.

Step #1: Protein Always Comes First

The first move to monitoring your keto diet macros effectively measures your protein intake. The sum will vary, depending on the level of action per person. When sedentary, eat at least 0.8 g of protein per lbs. of lean body mass.

Lean body mass is the weight you bear but is not fat. To find your lean body mass, using a bioelectric impedance meter or get a DEXA scan.

Take the weight then multiply this by 0.8. It is the sum of protein that every day you will eat. Consume 1-1.2 g of protein per lbs. of body weight whether you're an athlete or attempting to build muscle. That's the minimum amount that you should eat. If required, you can eat more, but you shouldn't worry about excess glucose production. Gaining less protein is more worrying than eating more.

Stage #2: Carbohydrate calculation

Reduce your overall carb intake to 20-50g. Athletes, as well as those looking for muscle building, should eat higher quantities, whereas those living a sedentary lifestyle will aim to remain below 30g of total carbs.

Chapter 3: Ketogenic Diet plan

To begin with a keto diet plan, everything you have to know includes tons of high-fat, low-carbohydrate recipe ideas. So, you have chosen to try the high-fat, low-carb diet, better known as the ketogenic diet that burns fat. Whether it is to lose weight, have far more energy, or just have energy workouts, going keto is a popular choice right now. Although figuring out your keto diet program is no easy feat, mainly because eating a diet that is pretty high in fats naturally doesn't come to several people who seem to be attached to the usually heavy-carb American food. (It's tough unless you're vegan and still want to follow keto.) And this should support: Keto experts clarify how to give yourself a chance for success, plus include suggestions on precisely what keto foods to consume when you begin. There's one aspect all experts agree on when it comes to starting the ketogenic diet (and any other diet for that matter). It is especially important to ensure that your keto diet strategy is very well considered out when you consume this way since the foods you could select are restricted.

3.1 Which ketogenic diet should you follow?

You often need to experiment with different versions of the ketogenic diet to achieve the best results based on your objectives and activity levels. For instance, if you exercise consistently at high-intensities, you can be struggling with your workouts after you begin to limit carbs. In such a case, it could be easier for you to utilize carbs as a performance-boosting tool, and the safest way to do that is to use a cyclical ketogenic diet or even a targeted ketogenic diet. Before we figure out which dietary strategy will be better for you, though, let's go over each one briefly.

Keto diet comes in three main styles:

- Standard Ketogenic Diet (SKD)
- Cyclical Ketogenic Diet (CKD)
- Targeted Ketogenic Diet (TKD)

Each of which provides a particular purpose for specific persons. You'll reap from one combination more than others, based on your objectives, your fitness routine, and your workout experience.

The Standard Ketogenic Diet

The Standard Keto Diet (SKD) is what many people consider when we talk about a keto diet. This is a low carbohydrate diet, mild in protein, as well as high in fat. If you are looking for fast fat loss and do only low to gentle intensity workouts (e.g., walk, yoga, cycling, and light weight lifting), then maybe the SKD could be the best diet for you.

For this approach to diet, carbs have to be significantly limited. A daily intake of 30 g or less of carbohydrates is usually needed to trigger and remain in ketosis (that is one of the main reasons for so much reducing carb intake). Keto carb restrictions differ from person to person. However, the basic rule is to avoid nuts, added sugars, and other high-carbon foods. Low carb beans, seeds, nuts, and high-fat dairy will be your primary drivers of carbs on the SKD. Check out our keto food page for a more in-depth look at what you'll find on the SKD.

The Targeted Keto Diet

The Targeted Ketogenic Diet (TKD) comprises of eating carbohydrates around exercise times (typically 30-60 min before) & at any other time following the SKD. The TKD gives us an easy way of maintaining high-intensity workout performance as well as facilitate glycogen depletion over extended periods without disrupting ketosis.

Usually, this dietary approach is recommended for two different groups of people: (1) individuals who need carbohydrates to fuel their workout performance but are unable or unwilling to take part in a CKD's long carb loads or (2) individuals who are just beginning an exercise routine and are reluctant to do the amount of physical activity required to maximize a CKD diet; If you're performing just cardio style exercises or any exercise that's low to mild in strength, then maybe the TKD (as well as CKD) isn't for you— then stick to the SKD.

The Cyclical Ketogenic Diet

The Cyclical Ketogenic Diet (CKD) is a nutritional method incorporating the day(s) of carb-loading with the traditional keto diet. This is usually used by those who are much more experienced when it comes to exercising at high intensity. Bodybuilders & athletes are a perfect example of a person who can use the CKD, as their training requires a high volume & intensity to improve their output. For this great amount and strength, without any of the help of carbs, it is almost difficult for them to practice at their peak.

For this purpose, it is best for them to introduce carbohydrate refeed days once or maybe twice a week to completely replenish glycogen stocks in order to power their training bouts with a sufficient amount of sugar.

Not like the TKD, in which the primary aim is to maintain a moderate level of blood sugar or muscle glycogen for exercise, the CKD's objective is to completely replenish glycogen throughout carb loads and replenish glycogen and raise ketone levels during carb loads. Both dietary strategies will, therefore, enable you to take advantage of carbs and ketosis.

What diet can you use?

There are some easy rules you must follow when it comes to choosing the correct keto diet for you.

If you never do exercise of high intensity, and only want to lose weight, stay with the SKD. Including more carbs to your diet only delays your development and keeps you out of ketosis.

You can advantage from the CKD as well as the TKD for all of you who regularly do training at high levels of intensity. Usually, we suggest that workout newcomers (i.e., persons who have been in high-intensity training for less than a year) seek the TKD, but they can only continue with it if they experience a substantial drop in results when on the SKD. All those who are more sophisticated with higher volumes of their coaching and training may be better off at the CKD. Nevertheless, bear in mind these are not strict regulations. Experimentation is crucial as it comes to finding out if CKD or TKD is better for you. Nobody is the same, and you need to see which works perfectly for you. Many people think various variants of a CKD are better, while others think the TKD to more reliably help them out. It helps you to have more flexibility in choosing what fits best. You can also try remaining on the SKD or changing your exercise schedule. High-intensity exercise is possible without the need for extra carbohydrates for success. To know how to do this despite losing muscle or strength, check out our Keto bodybuilding guide.

The only strict rule you must adopt is this: If you do not regularly exercise at high-intensity, you should adhere to the SKD. Most people just need an SKD diet. The CKD & TKD should be used to enhance the efficiency of heavy-intensity exercise and cannot be used as a justification for eating anything sweet before every workout. If you don't "hit the wall" with your training on a weekly basis, there's really no need to include carbs to your diet. CKD, as well as TKD, are for people pushing their bodies to the limitations, and not just for the suppression of craving.

Which Diet May Give You the Perfect Results?

People who are interested in certain versions of a keto diet usually ask which would show them best results – SKD, CKD or TKD. There's no clear answer to this because it's all dependent on the biology, training schedule, consumption of macronutrients, and caloric intake. In the end, with the same caloric intake, an SKD, CKD, and TKD may result in equal fat loss. The sum of muscle mass you are gaining (or keeping) also relies on your intake of protein, genetics, and a number of workouts. For instance, if implementing the SKD prevents you from exercising with as much frequency as you do before if you do want to build muscle and power, a CKD or TKD would be a better choice. However, if you don't fulfill your food requirements first & foremost, none of those diets would be helpful to you.

Any Ketogenic Diet's most significant part: Your nutritional needs.

Among the first important things to remember in any diet, and the most crucial is fulfilling your dietary needs. To do this, you'll want to ensure that you eat the right number of calories as well as macronutrients. The best way to know what your specifications are is to use a keto calculator.

Typically, if you want to lose weight, deduct from Total Energy Expenditure (TEE) measurement 10-15 percent of your calories. If muscle development is one of your objectives, increasing your calorie by 10-15 percent of your TEE. Only pretty easy, right? Okay, it's a little complex than that.

You need to get your macronutrients into action to make sure that you reach the targeted number. If you seek to build muscle mass in your exercises, the intake of protein will end up at the higher end of the scale (and could be higher than that for certain people).

As long as the protein intake does not interfere with ketosis, you're on the right path. Conversely, if you struggle to get into the ketosis, therefore dialing down the protein intake can work a little bit for you. You may eat once every day, two times a day, or nine times a day–just make sure you're drinking sufficient water and reaching your macros. Getting to know your water & macro needs is substantially more critical than timing the nutrients (For more information on how to time your intake of for optimal performance, check out our post on the topic.) When your body approaches ketosis, it will begin using ketones as the primary energy source (instead of glucose). Though studies indicate that ketones & fats are more effective for the body for using, most people find that without eating sufficient carbs (this is the whole idea behind utilizing the CKD and TKD), they never achieve their peak efficiency. If you'd like to understand why we need carbs to fuel some exercises, look up our keto as well as the exercise guide.

Bringing everything together — how would You Start?

Because most people here will use the SKD, there are four simple steps to start successfully: measure your caloric needs (TEE) and deduct or attach calories based on your objectives. Set the levels of protein to your targets. 0.8–1 g of lean muscle mass protein each pound is a healthy starting point—set carb concentrations.

Generally, about 20-30 g of net carbohydrates per day (less than 20 g is ideal during the first few weeks if you don't exercise). Set levels of fat consumption according to how much calories you left.

Note that the fats are 9 kcal/gram, 4 kcal/gram of protein, and 4 kcal/gram of carbs. Or you can use our keto calculator to do all the calculations you need. Using our keto-food guide to help you find out what to eat when you meet your macronutrient requirements.

For those of you who regularly train at high intensities and notice a significant decrease in quality while on the SKD, you'll most benefit from either of these three suggestions: trying to follow the targeted ketogenic diet (TKD). This works better typically for beginners with a high-intensity workout. Implement a Cyclic Ketogenic Diet (CKD) version that works with your schedule. This usually works stronger for athletes of high intensity or for bodybuilders who have been practicing for a few years. Sticking to the SKD and modifying your training, so you don't perform high-intensity workouts involving so much fuel carbs. Check our Guide to Keto Bodybuilding for more detailed recommendations. When the TKD or CKD sounds attractive to you, then maybe you can have a detailed look at TKD and a detailed look at CKD to determine what's right for you.

3.2 Plan your meals

It may seem daunting to turn to a ketogenic diet, but it does not have to be challenging. The attention will be on raising the carbohydrates while raising the meals & snacks ' fat and protein content. Carbs must be limited to enter and stay in a state of ketosis. Though some people can only get ketosis by consuming less than 20 g of carbs a day, others may be effective with a much high intake of carb. Typically speaking, the less the intake of carbohydrates, the easier it's to enter and remain in ketosis. That is why committing to keto-friendly meals and eliminating carbohydrate-rich products is the easiest way of losing weight on a keto diet.

Keto-friendly food to eat

Meals and snacks will focus on the following foods when adopting a ketogenic diet:

- Eggs: organic whole eggs make a much better option.
- Poultry: Turkey and Chicken.
- Fatty fish: Salmon, herring & mackerel.
- Meat: Beef fed with grass, pork, organ meat, and bison.
- Full-fat dairy: milk and sugar, butter.
- Full-fat cheese: mozzarella, cheddar, brie, goat cheese, and cream cheese.
- Nuts & seeds: Almonds and walnuts, pumpkin seeds, peanuts, and chia seeds.
- Nut butter: raw butter with peanut, almond & cashew.
- Good fats: olive oil, coconut oil, avocado oil, butter with coconut and sesame oil.
- Avocados: You can add whole avocados to almost every meal or snack.

- Vegetables that are not starchy: onions, tomatoes, mushrooms & peppers.
- Condiments: Lemon juice, pepper, salt, vinegar, fresh herbs & spices.

Foods to Avoid

Avoid carbohydrate-rich foods when adopting a keto diet.

There will be limits on the following foods:

- Bread & baked goods: white bread, whole wheat bread, cookies, doughnuts, and rolls.
- Sweets and sugars: sugar, ice-cream, sweets, maple syrup, and sugar from coconut.
- Sweetened drinks: coffee, juice, sweetened teas, and sports drinks.
- Pasta: Noodles and Spaghetti.
- Grain items: wheat, rice, beans, cereals for tea, and tortillas.
- Starchy vegetables: carrots, sweet potatoes, squash with butternut, beans, peas, and pumpkin.
- Beans & legumes: black beans, lentils, chickpeas, and kidney beans.
- Fruit: Orange, apples, pineapple, and bananas.
- High-carbohydrate sauces: Barbecue sauce, dressings for sugar salads, and sauces for dipping.
- Some alcoholic drinks: blended beer and sugar.

While carbs should be limited, low-glycemic fruits like berries may be experienced in limited quantities as long as you maintain a keto-friendly range of macronutrients. Choose safe food sources and avoid fried foods & unhealthy fats. The following things should be avoided: Margarine, compressing, and vegetable oils like canola and corn oil are unhealthy fats. Meat processed: Fast food, frozen meals, and processed meats, including hot dogs, lunch meats — Diet foods: foods containing artificial colors including sugar alcohols and aspartame, preservatives as well as sweeteners.

Keto-Friendly Beverages

Sugar can be used in a wide range of beverages like juice, soda, iced tea, and coffee. High-carb beverages must be avoided while on a keto diet, just as high-carb foods are. It is no small matter that sugar drinks were also related to numerous health problems — from obesity to increased diabetes risk. Fortunately for anyone on the keto diet, there are several tasty, sugar-free options. Keto-friendly drink options include:

- Water: Water is the perfect hydration option and should be drunk all day long.
- Sparkling water: The sparkling water can be an ideal substitute for soda.
- Unsweetened coffee: Try to apply heavy cream to your cup of joe.
- Green tea without sweetening: Green tea is tasty and offers many benefits for people.

Whenever you want to add extra taste to your tea, consider playing with various variations of keto-friendly flavors. Tossing a little fresh mint as well as the lemon peel in your water bottle, for example, can make staying hydrated a breeze? While alcohol should be limited, sometimes having a low-carb drink such as vodka or tequila combined with soda water is absolutely fine.

Healthy choices for ketogenic snack

Eating between meals can help reduce hunger, when adopting a ketogenic diet, and keep you on track. Since the ketogenic diet is so satisfying, depending on your level of activity, you might only need one or two snacks a day. Here are some excellent options for the keto-friendly snack:

- Almonds & cheddar cheese.
- Half avocado stuffed with chicken salad.
- Guacamole, with veggies low in carb.
- Trail mixture made of unsweetened coconut, nuts, and seeds.
- Hard-boiled eggs.
- Coconut chips.
- Kale chips.
- Sliced salami and olives.
- Celery and peppers with a dip of herb cream cheese.
- Berries with heavy whipping cream.
- Jerky.
- Cheese roll-ups.
- Parmesan crisps.
- Macadamia nuts.
- Greens with a dressing rich in fat with avocado.

- Keto smoothie made from milk of coconut, cocoa, and avocado.
- Avocado cocoa mousse.

While these keto snacks are capable of maintaining fullness between meals, they can also lead to weight gain if you eat too much all day. It's essential to eat the right number of calories depending on your level of exercise, weight loss target, gender, and age. When you're uncertain how many calories you may consume, check out this article to learn how to measure the energy requirements.

A balanced ketogenic diet would consist of around 75% fat, 20% protein, and just 5% or less than 50g of carbohydrates per day. Make your focus on high-fat and low-carb foods such as eggs, meats, dairy as well as low-carb vegetables, and sugar-free drinks. Be sure to avoid highly processed products and fats that are unhealthy. The ketogenic diet's popularity has made finding a wide array of exciting and nutritious keto meal ideas online simpler than ever before Using this chapter as a guide to starting the keto diet can set you for success and make a breeze on transitioning to a high-fat, low-carb diet.

3.3 The 30 days keto diet plan guideline

The quantities of fat and protein should be enough for most ordinary people to keep you satiated naturally and keep you in a caloric deficit, naturally. Yet the American average is often not normal. There are plenty of issues with the hormone, the endocrine, and the deficiency that we have to remember. That said, when you are eating more than your own body is spending, it doesn't always enable you to lose weight. "Macros" is an abbreviated form of macronutrient. These are the "big three"-fats, carbohydrates, and proteins. You may use a calculator to figure out how many or how little of each of the milestones you need to reach.

The calculator can be found on the site's navigation panel! Many people take the macros as something of a "set in stone" kind. You shouldn't care regarding hitting the target to your dot every other day. If you're a couple of calories for a few days, a couple of calories down on some–that's great. All will finally come out except for itself. It's all about a strategy that will work for you in the long run and not the way around. I wanted to put it out that I actually designed this meal plan with the women in mind. I took about 150 women on average, and what their macros were. The end result was 1600 calories-divided into 136 g of fat, 74 g of protein, and 20 g of net carbs a day. Like most of us live, this is all built around a sedentary lifestyle. It's pretty easy to increase calories - increase the amount of fat you consume.

Coconut oil, olive oil, macadamia nuts, and butter are perfect ways to raise fats without having too much from the other stuff in the way. Drizzle it over salads, slather it over vegetables, snack it on, do what you have to do to make this work for you! You'll have to worry about what you have to do to cut calories. You'll most likely need less protein too. Therefore, bear in mind sections of meal sizes. Reduce them as needed, or to see fit. Last but not least, they stick to the plan! Ketosis is a mechanism that takes place within your body. You can't have a cheat meal just for "that one." If you are doing, it can hinder progress for a week until your body gets back into ketosis and usually works again. You would like to keep your cheats to no other. Be prepared, ensure that you consume anything you need to be sated ("full"), and make sure that you are pleased with what you consume. When you have to compel yourself to eat it, that's never going to work out. It is just a guide about how to eat a ketogenic diet, and you're welcome to change what kind of food you consume!

Week 1:

Our primary goal here, at first, is to remain quite simple. Simplicity is key in my mind for someone who is just beginning a low carb diet. You don't want this to be a tough change (kitchen-wise), as even getting rid of your hunger would be hard. Leftovers could be another matter that we must take into account. It's not only easier for you, however why put yourselves through the hassle of more than once cooking the same food? The first symptoms of ketosis are known as "keto flu," where brain fogginess, headaches, tiredness, etc. can really rile up the body. Make sure you drink more than enough water and eat lots of salt. The keto diet is a natural stimulant, and you're going to pee beyond normal. Take into consideration that you're peeing out electrolytes, and you can say you're going to have a thumping pain in head in no time. It is very important to keep your salt intake as well as water intake high enough so that your body can re-hydrate & re-supply your electrolytes. Doing so will relieve the headaches if it does not absolutely get rid of them. Drink the water with a salt sprinkling in it, if you need to. Only continue drinking water and continue to consume salt. Trust me; it would help. If you are concerned about the salt and high blood pressure, don't be! Recent research shows that sodium intake, as well as blood pressure, aren't as associated as we once believed.

Breakfast

You have to do something for breakfast that's simple, convenient, tasty, and will, of course–give you the leftovers. I recommend starting day 1 on the weekend. That way, you could make that will last you all week long.

The first week relates to convenience. Before work, no one wants to have breakfast, and we will not do that either!

Lunch

Here too, we'll keep it easy. It'll be salad and meat most of the time, coated in high-fat sauces and making it a day. Here we're not going to get too unruly. You can use the leftover meat through previous nights or conveniently accessible chicken/fish canned. Try reading the labels if you are using canned meats to find the one that contains the minimum (or no) contaminants!

Dinner

Dinner would be a mix of leafy greens with some meat (usually broccoli & spinach). We're going to go up on the fat again, and medium on the protein.

Week 2:

Breakfast.

We are now going to mix it up a little for breakfast. It is here that we present keto proof coffee. Now, don't misunderstand me-I know some of you won't like it. If you aren't a coffee fan, then try tea. If you're not a taste fan (which is very rare), then try to make a mixture of the ingredients by yourself and eat it this way. Why, then, keto proof coffee? The Loss of Fat. Clear and easy, the intake of medium-chain triglycerides (MCT) has been shown to result in greater losses in both animal and human adipose tissue (fat tissue).

Fats! May I even describe this one? It has been shown that consuming fat results in greater quantities of energy, more efficient use of resources, and more significant weight loss. It's the key element of the diet, not to mention—more Energy. Studies have also shown that the rapid oxidation rate in MCFAs (Medium Chain Fatty Acids) contributes to a rise in energy spending. MCFAs are primarily transformed into ketones (our best friends), absorbed in a different manner in the body as compared to regular oils, as well as overall give us more energy.

If you're not the fan of the flavor, feel free to apply sweetener and spices to this—Cinnamon, Vanilla extract, etc. Everything you like is a great tasting. Every day you can even turn the taste so you won't get bored! If this is your first keto proof coffee drinking, I recommend you take 1-2 hours or so to drink it down. Generally, when people have a large exposure to coconut oil and are not used to it, it can very often cause them to go to the bathroom. Make sure you build coconut oil tolerance before you drink it within a 20-minute time frame.

Lunch.

We're always here to keep simple. We may add more meat from the previous cooking night into any lunch that we do. Green vegetables and dressings high in fat (or vinaigrettes) are essential. Ensuring that the fats are matched with the protein quantities is very critical.

Dinner.

Dinner, again, is going to be quite simple. Meat, vegetables, high-fat dressings are the core of our lives. Perhaps even a caking of butter on our fruits, as we get friskier.

Don't think things over in the first 2 weeks; success is easy.

Week 3:

Breakfast.

With breakfast, we are going full-on fats just like we did last week. This time we're going to double the quantity of keto proof coffee (or tea) we're drinking, which means we are doubling the amount of coconut oil, butter & heavy cream. It is expected to come up with quite a lot of calories, which will probably keep us full for dinner. Need to keep on drinking water like some kind of fiend to make sure that you remain hydrated.

Lunch.

No lunch, oh no! Don't worry-the morning fats will keep you feeling complete and energized till the lunch. Normally people start to hit a wall at about 2 pm at first, so make sure to have plenty of water to drink.

Dinner.

Alright, dinner remains the same. Vegetables, Meat, and fats will almost always be the standard for dinnertime. But don't worry-we're going to mix things in some bread-y stuff!

Week: 4

Breakfast.

We are on the fast! Black coffee, if you're a caffeine addict. Tea, if you're not that much into the coffee. Like coffee, tea can have great health benefits too. Two of the great advantages of green tea are Polyphenols–These work in your body as antioxidants.

Epigallocatechin gallate (EGCG) is the strongest antioxidant in green tea, which has been shown to be powerful against fatigue. Enhanced brain function–Green tea not only contains caffeine, but it also includes L-theanine, an amino acid. L-theanine improves the GABA function, thus boosting waves of anxiety, dopamine & alpha. Improved metabolic rate-It has been shown that green tea can increase the metabolic rate. This can result in up to 15 percent increased fat oxidation in association with caffeine.

Lunch.

Water and then a little more water. You can't eat lunch, and you can't eat the meal. So, make sure you remain hydrated Usually. Whether you do a decent job with your hydration is important here. Recall-I suggests 4 liters a day.

Dinner.

Lots and tons of dessert food to fill the bases! Dinner is a wonderful time for me. I recommend you break your fast with just a small snack, then eat to your heart's content after 30-45 minutes. I usually need 2 meals to get to my macros, and I guess you'll have to do the same thing.

Week: 5

This is where we will end! I'm sorry to say that you are isolated. You will have plenty of preserved leftovers, ready and waiting! I know many of you here have problems with scheduling and thus are busy–so make sure that it's important to freeze those nights you're doing extras. Do you have all those leftovers in your freezer? Using them! Make your own diet plan, first use this as a reference, then do it yourself entirely. It will be easy until you get the grasp of it.

3.4 days balanced keto-meal plan

A 7-Day Keto Diet Sample Menu.

Day one:

Breakfast: Scrambled buttered eggs on a bed of lettuce with avocado on top.

Snack: Sunflower seeds.

Lunch: Spinach salad with smoked salmon.

Snack: Bits of celery & pepper plunged into guacamole.

Dinner: cauliflower mashed pork chop with red cabbage slaw.

Day two.

Breakfast: Bulletproof coffee (made with coconut oil and butter), hard-boiled eggs.

Snack: Macadamia nuts.

Lunch: Tuna salad, filled with tomatoes.

Snack: roast beef and roll-ups with sliced cheese.

Dinner: meatballs served with cream sauce on zucchini noodles.

Day three.

Breakfast: veggie omelet & cheese served with salsa.

Snack: Full-fat Greek yogurt and crushed pecans.

Lunch: take-out sashimi with miso soup.

Snack: Almond milk smoothie, greens, almond butter, and protein powder.

Dinner: Asparagus-roasted chicken and sautéed mushrooms.

Day four.

Breakfast: Smoothie made with almond milk, vegetables, almond butter & protein powder.

Snack: Two hard-boiled eggs.

Lunch: chicken tender made with almond flour on a bed of cucumbers and goat cheese.

Snack: sliced cheese as well as bell pepper slices

Dinner: grilled shrimp served with a lemon butter sauce with asparagus side

Day five.

Breakfast: Bacon scrambled eggs as well as a side of vegetables.

Snack: A pinch of berries with something like a quarter-cup of walnuts.

Lunch: Grass-fed burger served with avocado and a side salad in a lettuce "bun."

Snack: sticks of celery coated in almond butter.

Dinner: Baked tofu with cauliflower rice, broccoli, and peppers, with a peanut sauce on top.

Day six.

Breakfast: Baked eggs in cups made with avocado.

Snack: Kale chips.

Lunch: Rolls of poached avocado salmon wrapped in (rice-free) seaweed.

Snack: a bar made from meat (Turkey or pork).

Dinner: Grilled beef kebabs and sautéed broccolini with peppers.

Day seven.

Breakfast: Scrambled eggs with veggies, with salsa on top.

Snack: Strips of dried seaweed and cheese.

Lunch: Sardine salad in half an avocado, filled with mayo.

Snack: Turkey jerky (have no sugars added).

Dinner: Broiled buttered trout, sautéed bok choy.

Chapter 4: Ketogenic diet for women

The keto diet is based on a routine that is very low in carb. Carbs are generally reduced to less than 50 grams a day, often supplemented with fat & moderate protein amounts. When you're in a diet or weight loss discussion, you'll probably hear about the ketogenic diet or keto diet. This is because the ketogenic diet has become one of the world's most common methods for losing excess weight as well as improving health. As a general rule, the keto diet is very low in carbohydrates, high in fat, and medium in protein. Carbohydrates are reduced to less than 50g a day when adopting a ketogenic diet, but there are more strict and loose variations of the diet. Fats must replace most cut carbs, and provide around 75% of your caloric intake. Proteins will account for approximately 20% of energy needs, while carbs are typically limited to 5%. This reduction in carb causes the body to rely on fats instead of glucose as its main source of the energy-a process known as ketosis. When in ketosis, the body uses ketones, molecules made from fats in the liver when glucose is limited — as such, an alternative source of fuel. While fat is often avoided due to its high-calorie count, the study shows that keto diets are far more successful than low-fat diets in encouraging weight loss. In addition, ketogenic diets minimize appetite and improve satiety, which can be especially useful when attempting to lose weight.

4.1 Why weight loss is difficult for women?

A husband and wife seek to lead a healthy lifestyle. By eating healthy, and joining a nearby gym, they inspire and support one another. They work together and do everything advised by their internal medicine physician. The husband has lost 10 pounds after three months.

The wife, five. How the results are different if they practiced the same routine. Female has always assumed that weight loss was easier for men and science confirms this view.

According to research carried out in the Yale Journal of Biology & Medicine, being female-only doubles the risk of becoming overweight. Western women are 3.3% more likely to be overweight than their male counterparts, and 3% more likely to be obese. This gets worse if you find those numbers are disturbing. The research also shows that women are more likely than men to die from diseases linked to weight. Health-related issues arise in women at a lower BMI relative to men. Females are 6.6 times more likely than men to have a weight-related illness. The reasons for moving far beyond issues of diet and exercise, and concentrating on the hormonal & structural disparities between males and females.

1. Hormones are a big problem in women's weight loss.

Many people are losing muscle mass and gaining weight as they age. This shift isn't in the way the body utilizes calories, which can make weight loss hard. There is one extra difficulty for women: menopause. The post-menopausal female is more likely to have weight than men in the same age groups because of the drop in estrogen. Also, female hormones store calories as fat, which requires more space than lean muscles.

2. Metabolism.

Males and females have differing metabolisms. Men have a higher resting metabolic rate due to greater lean muscle mass. You read that correctly. Since the muscle consumes more calories than fat and sometimes doing nothing, the men burn more calories than the women. As if that wasn't enough, women store fat differently, too. Fat has an irritating tendency for ladies to gravitate to the hips, thighs, and buttocks — areas where losing is more difficult.

3. Emotion.

This is really true: as per a 2013 report published in American Journal of Clinical Nutrition, women appear to be more emotional munchers than men. The rationale behind the research, of course, was much more complex than only reaching for a chocolate bar while stressed. Females appear to have a lower metabolic rate than men by nature. This ensures that the body requires fewer calories (energy units) to power normal body processes, such as breathing, thought, and flowing blood. The calories leftover are processed as fat. Besides, the composition of the female body typically exceeds that of the males. In many other words, people prefer to put more muscle than fat on pounds, reducing the body mass index (BMI). Muscle, for men luckily, consumes greater calories than fat — at even rest. People have been asking for years, "Why females have a harder time losing weight?" Females have an easier time, physiologically, holding on to extra weight.

Genetic makeup is another metabolic factor that can make it more difficult for females to lose weight. Your mom and grandmother all had separate setpoints, which are abstract weight limits the body seeks to remain in. This fixed point is also passed on, which can work against your attempts to lose weight. Another gene that you have inherited is the shape of your body. Research has also shown that females with common body types (such as pear & apple) are at higher risk of becoming obese or overweight.

Many women seeking to lose weight want instant results. They prefer to eliminate whole food groups or raising calorie intake significantly for a faster weight loss.

As you already know, this strategy contributes to nutritional yo-yo, whereby temporary outcomes are counteracted as the weight returns — sometimes even more so than previously.

Incremental improvements in lifestyle all work to improve health and wellbeing. Every time you're wondering why it's easier for males to lose the weight, always remember: restaurants offer the same portion size, and the bartender serves another round for everyone. It depends on He is up to you to decide then stick to your special portion control.

4.2 Ketosis for women's health

The end goal of the ketogenic diet is ketosis. It is characterized as a metabolic state of increased ketone production and increased burning of fat. But it comes with most of health benefits, too. But ketosis apparently causes a number of adverse side effects for women. This causes many female keto-ers on the keto bandwagon to think twice before jumping.

It may seem like keto is interfering with female hormones, from menstrual irregularities to excessive weight gain. Are these problems just a consequence of ketosis, or is it anything else? The simple answer is, yes, ketosis may affect hormones in females. The broad answer is that so much of it depends on your eating habits and your wellbeing. There are several ways for women to troubleshoot ketosis so they can enjoy all of the advantages of keto safely.

If your body doesn't get enough glucose to produce energy, then it starts burning the fats. The effect is an accumulation of molecules, termed ketones. It's called ketosis when you have more ketones in your blood. These ketones are created by the mitochondria in your liver most often to fuel your brain. But when needed, even your muscles and heart may run on ketones.

Nature invented ketosis to help us survive in times of hunger. Luckily to go into ketosis, you don't have to starve. Scientists have discovered that merely reducing carbs to under 50 grams per day is enough to place you in such a metabolic state.

It is at the heart of ketogenic diets as well as higher consumption of fat to help you feel fresh and stimulated. However, beyond simple fat burning, ketosis has benefits. A broad systematic analysis of ketogenic studies reveals ketogenic diets:

- Cardiovascular health improvement.
- Control type 2 diabetes.
- Treats epilepsy.
- Reduces the risk of cancer.
- Treats PCOS.
- Treats brain disorders.

- And minimize acne.

There is clear evidence that keto improves mental and physical efficiency. Keto may seem like the next magic pill, with all these rewards to reap. But keto isn't all rainbows and sunshine; adverse effects on a keto diet do occur, and women find this diet extremely hard to adhere to.

Nutrition and Hormones:

For women, ketosis can be difficult as any nutritional changes have a huge impact on female hormones. In fact, the fine balance of sex hormones is strongly tied to the overall wellbeing of a woman; any disruption in this equilibrium is likely to cause trouble. Let's start by listing some brief information about how female sex hormones influence health to make you understand why it is so: Estrogen and progesterone influence your neurotransmitter levels, illustrating why variations in hormones affect mood, sleeping, & mental function.

- Estrogen is a central factor in the metabolism of the bone that decreases in this hormone raises the risk of osteoporosis in menopause.
- Progesterone levels are influencing thyroid hormones in your body.
- Estrogen supports your metabolism and cardiovascular health.
- Progesterone inhibits your immune system, particularly during pregnancy.

Your pituitary gland, a small gland at the base of your brain, controls the balance of these two main female sex hormones. Your lifestyle & diet, however, may also have a significant effect on that balance. In specific, here's how ketosis can influence your hormones:

- Ketosis reduces insulin levels, a pancreatic hormone that is necessary for the body to utilize glucose. Ketosis also raises leptin levels, an appetite-suppressing hormone.
- Eating 5 percent more fat than normal in women raises the levels of estrogen & androgen during menopause by 12 percent.
- Hypothalamic–pituitary–adrenal axis (HPA axis) is activated by ketosis. HPA axis relates to the hormonal activity of the hypothalamus, the pituitary as well as the adrenal glands.
- Research shows fasting, which can cause ketosis, raises cortisol levels, a stress hormone. That's how you see fasting as a danger to your health.
- Insulin sensitivity influences the balance of sex hormones profoundly. Ketosis may enhance your sensitivity to insulin.

Your thyroid gland health is also having an effect on your sexual health. For example, women with thyroid disorders frequently suffer from infertility as well as a deficiency in progesterone.

That's because thyroid disorders interfere with the functioning of the pituitary gland, so this gland begins reproductive & total hormonal health. The thyroid is particularly nutritionally sensitive.

Studies have found that low-calorie diets, as well as ketosis, can lead to a drop in some people's thyroid hormones. Those who eat roughly 50 grams of carbohydrates a day, though, do not seem to have these problems. Low levels of other thyroid hormones also minimize levels of the sex hormone-binding globulin (SHBG). This contributes to the development of more estrogen in your ovaries than required, causing heavy or prolonged periods. By contrast, the abnormally high levels of thyroid hormone increase SHBG, which causes light periods.

It is because ketosis and low-carb diets imitate appetite, and the thyroid gland responds to appetite by reducing those hormone levels. If this occurs to you, then you should try carbohydrate cycling or enhancing your fat consumption. The aim is to give your body sufficient energy to work on other than carbohydrates, and this will aid in stabilizing the functioning of the thyroid.

Ketosis for women

People on keto diets frequently note changes in menstruation. Many also claim that the diet doesn't help them lose weight, or even they have gained weight. Would that mean the ketogenic diet disrupts the female hormones, and it is not appropriate for female sex? Not exactly. The keto diet has the same powerful effect on male hormones as those on females. It's just that females identify the results more outwardly. Because of ketosis, women who experience menstrual disorders and weight gain on ketogenic diets do not usually go through such problems.

Here's what these issues may be causing: weight loss: Ketosis also leads to rapid weight loss that is nice if you start your keto journey when obese. Research shows that sharp weight losses trigger sharp estrogen drops. This, in effect, is triggering anovulation and the periods missing.

Low consumption of fat: Consuming more fat will raise levels of estrogen, right? Indeed, it is true, but you get used to making ketones with a lot of the fats you consume. When you eat too little fat in fear of weight gain, it can have a negative effect on your cycles.

Resistance to insulin: There's sufficient proof that variations in sex hormones change the sensitivity of insulin. Insulin sensitivity has an effect on the capacity of the body to use glucose. Not being insulin sensitive may lead to cravings for sugar as well as weight gain.

Not being in ketosis: You simply must make sure you don't eat more than 30g of net carbohydrates a day to get into ketosis. Otherwise, you fear to store all the excess fat you consume and triggering hormonal disturbance.

Stress: The keto diet should initially be stressful on your body, which can contribute to menstrual disruptions. So, when you are keto-adapted, the levels of cortisol will drop, and your menses should become normal. If this doesn't occur, the issue is, maybe, the outside stressors. And as far as women's ketosis study goes, several studies clearly indicate that it enhances women's health. There have been at least seven studies investigating the impact of keto on menstrual period, and all suggest that low-carb diets promote ovulation as well as menstrual regularity.

Ketosis for Females Benefits

Now we have discussed the possible downsides for women in ketosis; it is time to think about the rewards. Many women have more to gain from ketosis than others. Females who are overweight, sedentary, having PCOS, epilepsy, resistance to insulin, or any other health problems should certainly consider moving to keto.

Metabolic disorders, such as for overweight, PCOS, & diabetes, may well react to ketosis. This is because insulin, glucose, and weight are reduced by ketosis. High glucose & insulin levels, as well as excessive body weight, can conflict with your metabolism. More often than not, such issues stem from diets that are too high in dangerous carbohydrates, and poor in healthy fats. Ketosis may also stabilize menstrual disturbances in women suffering from PCOS. One research indicates that females with PCOS lost weight during 24 weeks of being on keto, had lower levels of testosterone, and had normal female hormones. So even if you do not suffer from any metabolic disorders, menstrual problems can occur when you are obese. When you have excessive body fat, the estrogen levels increase. It is because the fat tissue also acts as an endocrine organ releasing estrogen in fat cells. More fat you get, the more estrogen the body releases. Excessive Too much estrogen may make the symptoms of PMS worse.

Ketosis is healthy and even advantageous for women. Females with metabolic disorders such as obesity as well as PCOS benefit from ketosis. Ketosis causes them to remove extra body fat as well as improve the working of the metabolism that balances female hormones in turn.

Females who are particularly active, underweight, quickly lose weight, or fail to eat enough fats that experience menstrual disorders on a keto diet. This is because female sex hormone development is dependent on body fat & diet. Luckily, there have been ways to fix this problem. You will enjoy the advantages of ketosis without thinking about your sexual health by eating enough calories by not dropping too much weight and also by holding stress at bay. Research indicates that keto works just as well for women as it is for men. However, when you continue your keto adventure, you need to take into consideration the differences between men and women.

4.3 Sex difference – How a keto diet for women is different?

Researchers suggest this drastic disparity may be attributed to the predominant female sex hormone — estrogen, at least in part. They extracted some of the female mice's ovaries to study and performed a similar experiment. They were doing so substantially changed outcomes. Female mice without ovaries eating a keto diet reported a reduction in body fat compared with mice receiving a control diet, and they also retained regulation of blood glucose. In other words, the keto diet performed without Östrogen.

Cochran states, "This result indicates that postmenopausal women could have better weight loss results with the keto diet compared to younger women." Nevertheless, researchers make it very clear that it is necessary to talk to a doctor before beginning a keto diet.

This research is one of the few for examining possible gender gaps in keto diet effectiveness. The research, however, used an animal model, and scientists would also need to check out human studies before we can come to any firm conclusions.

Women are more subject to leptin sensitivity

The response to leptin (a satiety hormone) is one of the major disparities between males and females. Miller states that it is these leptin inequalities that most likely segregate males and females on a keto diet.

What she says is that in order to create ketones, a keto diet focuses on carb restriction, which, in effect, reduces leptin hormone. Females have thyroid leptin receptors in their ovaries, and they have a much greater sensitivity to leptin than men do.

It may be a concern since, over time, too low leptin levels can affect anxiety, insomnia & hunger. And menstruating females who live a high-stress lifestyle are, according to Miller, especially vulnerable to this discrepancy in leptin on a keto diet. "It may mess with the development of thyroid hormones, throw off the cycle of a female and inhibit the development of hormones," describes Miller. This being said, women can need to be eating more carbohydrates strategically than men.

The good news is, menstruating women may use the menstrual cycle as a sign of being A-okay to their bodies when practicing keto. "Menstrual cycles for women are genuinely a controlling sign that the body is healthy or balanced," says Miller. And, if the menstrual cycle of a woman is more erratic than normal, it may be an indication that her body does not react well to keto or that her level of leptin is too small.

This is when starting carbohydrate cycling may be helpful, according to Miller.

"I see a huge variation in women who sometimes need carbohydrate cycling, particularly if they're in low body fat, they workout and they're not sleepy enough," she adds. Women may want to boost their carbohydrate intake during carb cycling (while on keto!) to guarantee that their levels of leptin do not get too low. So, bear in mind if you're feeling nervous, chronically hungry, or even just generally off when on keto.

Women's commitment can become harmful.

For almost all other situations, persistence is an inspiring, redeeming performance— too many ladies Miller sees for her work have, and do so diligently, this overwhelming desire to achieve their aims.

When it comes to keto, however, Miller says that sometimes this consistency can do more damage than good.

With all the leptin deficiency & hormone disruption that can occur with uncontrolled keto, female bodies may not feel healthy enough to bear a child, contributing to the loss of their menstrual cycle. Miller also sees this type of customer. "Women who type-A go-getters, who just want to do all the stuff, and who simply don't have too much weight to lose — it maybe three to five lbs, or even a pure shift in composition," she tells me. "If they fast, as well as strict carb control, their leptin levels mostly decline, and even the body says,' I'm not healthy.'" So, this perfectionist tendencies that can occur with keto may have a dark side. People need to know when so much is actually so much to keep their hormones balanced — a word of caution that we can extend to men too, but particularly to women pursuing a keto-eating program. Although both males and females can reap tremendous benefits from a ketogenic diet, keeping those differences in mind is crucial. You will keep a healthy and successful personalized eating plan by understanding these variations and modifying keto to help determine your particular hormones & hunger levels.

4.4 How to make keto diet effective for women?

A women's keto diet doesn't have to be a failure for the body — it may be the best decision for your wellbeing. Let's continue with the biggest tip here you will have to follow to work first with a keto diet:

#1: Limit your carbohydrates slowly.

Unlike the males who can decide to start a keto diet every random day and go from 300 g daily carbohydrates in the Standard American Diet to 25 g, women need some more time to adapt, as we have discussed.

If you have not yet adopted a keto diet, continue by keeping up on your daily intake of food. This would not only give you opportunities to calculate your food and monitor your macros in keto, but this will also provide you with an average level of carb for your body. Let's presume you're a normal American girl who eats 250 g of carbs a day. While the fewer carbs you consume can get through ketosis quicker, achieving success does not require drastic steps. As 24 women adopted an eight-week low carbohydrate diet, they lost a mean of 19 pounds and reported substantial decreases in blood sugar, insulin resistance, triglyceride levels & free testosterone levels simply by reducing their net carbohydrates to 70 g a day. That demonstrates you don't need to stay just off the bat under 25 g to see the output. Use this roadmap to move your hormones in low-carb living: Week 1 of your keto diets will begin with a target of no further than 150 g of net carbs per day. Whether you can finish anywhere near a 100 g mark per day this first week. Do the same thing on week 2 of your keto diet; start about 100 g early this week, and end nearly 50 g daily. You'll be well on the way to the under-25 g region either close or in ketosis by the 3rd week. This reduction in carb will allow your body to change and adapt while seeing what life with fewer carbs is like. Just try to ensure to know your body.

When you're feeling sluggish, not able to complete your workouts, and are always hungry, you might need to include a few additional carbs to your day till you're fat adapted. The next tip works well for breaking stalls of weight loss.

#2: Try Intermittent Fasting.

How are females busting ASAP by their evolutionary fat reserves and kickstart weight loss? And sporadic acceleration.

Intermittent fasting is that when you go 14–18 hours without consuming any meals or snacks.

The most popular form of intermittent fasting (IF) is the 16/8 type; that is when you, re fasting for 16 hours of the day and consume only during a given 8-hour period. Intermittent fasting gives body a break from tiring work of digesting food items. The body should work on restoring itself while regulating the hormones throughout this down period, rather than going through digestive rigamarole. So, when the body completes all these things and is a little peckish, it's going to use your fat stores for fuel, so you don't get more than you use. Fasting enables you to get to ketosis more easily, and you lose weight faster. In only two months, one research found that over 84 percent of respondents exercising was having major weight loss performance. IF also retains muscle mass, thus facilitating loss of pure fat. For another experiment, when participants were divided into groups, they ate the same number of calories; however, some used IF, and others missed it. Scientists found that IF participants had not only lost a lot of weight, they retained their muscles and then lost pure fat. Because we know that muscles improve the metabolism and consume more calories when at rest, it's a double whammy of grandeur.

Studies also indicate that intermittent fasting will reduce the risk of your:

- heart disease.
- Cholesterol levels.

Inflammation.

And investigators had women prolong their overnight fasting in one study of nearly 2,500 ladies and discovered: people fasting fewer than 13 hours had such a higher risk of breast cancer relative to those who fasted for 13 hours or more.

Rising 2-hour increase in fasting has been linked to lower sugar levels as well as long night sleep.

Eating a light dinner before 8 pm is the best way to get into intermittent fasting, slipping in for a full night's rest, and also not eating when you wake up till you reach the required 14-hour fasting goal. As you are expected to get eight hours of sleep a night, by the time you get up, you are already midway into your fasting part. Attempt to fast every second day. Do not perform long runs, HIIT, or heavy workouts during this time because most likely; you will burn out. Consider yoga instead, or do regular walks with your pet.

#3: Learn How to Wisely Consume Your PMS Cravings.

Whenever it refers to PMS cravings, we are not all the same, but usually, people dream of candy, sugar, and high-calorie fast food during this time of the month. Actually, attempt any one of these keto recipe ideas for PMS whenever the storm hits:

Sweet:

- Keto Bars.
- Homemade Healthy Keto Choco Bars.
- Chocolate Keto Chia Pudding.
- Chocolate Mint Keto Ice Cream.
- Keto Chocolate Mug Cake.
- Keto Brownies, with Crunch Peppermint.
- Chocolate Chip Keto Cookies.
- Chocolate Sea Salt Peanut Butter Bites.

Salty:

- Crispy Kale Chips.
- Creamy Keto Cauliflower Mac & Cheese.
- Keto Jalapeño Poppers.
- Creamy Keto Spinach Artichoke Dip.
- Celeriac Everything Oven Fries.

But stay far away from the scale for your emotional and mental wellbeing, before & during your period time. However, try not to skip the gym-after all, exercise helps with cramps.

#4: Add Resistance Training.

Building muscles intentionally won't turn you into some kind of jacked meathead. This can improve your metabolism by getting more muscles, burn several calories at rest, even make your body look much better whilst not losing weight. In a four-week experiment of 45 sedentary females with PCOS, and that's no simple feat, resistance training even contributed to the improved reproductive process and reduced belly fat. So, exercise 20–30 min with dumbbells at least two times a week.

#5: Monitor Your Food consumption and Carry a Keto Journal.

You'll need to watch your intake of food on keto to ensure sure you hit all your macros (don't go over your carbohydrates or protein). You might want to utilize a food tracking software to manage all of those measurements. Yet you must also try keeping a journal on keto. Because the female body is so responsive to changes, you may use this room to record how you experience in keto life. You should be able to track stats and adjustments such as you're:

- Body goals.
- Weight.
- Body measurements.
- Workouts.
- Moods and emotions.
- Energy levels.
- Exercise recovery.
- Cravings.

Even if you do not feel like monitoring all of this material, it will be incredibly helpful in the long run for your gyno or doctor. You can be able to identify habits that you don't handle well, or maybe even food. And if your body needs additional supplements, you will have a greater understanding of which ones will be of greatest help.

#6: Take into account Keto-Friendly Supplements.

Females are more likely to have urinary tract infections (UTIs); however, the prevention and cure of go-to cranberry juice have far too much sugar to be keto-friendly.

Don't avoid taking that effective antioxidant; only consider a low-carb cranberry extraction supplement that you can pop up with for the same advantage. For improved hair, nails, eyes, joints & digestion, you should include collagen protein in your diet too. If you don't know any of the collagen advantages, now's the time to search out. Exogenous ketones may help you get to ketosis quicker when you just begin keto diet or come off a break day, so they rank highly as one of the strongest keto supplements to buy.

You're prepared to take control over your life and to get started with all this knowledge on keto for ladies! Although keto for women requires a little more preparation and consideration to get perfect, it can be the best choice you'll ever make for your fitness, beauty, and well-being.

4.5 Mistakes women do during keto diet

Particularly for women, there have been so many variables that come into play, because we undergo changes on a monthly basis in sex hormones.

That means that at certain points of the month, you can consume more food, undergo fluid retention, mood changes, and more! Perhaps you may experience underlying health issues such as diabetes, chronic fatigue, and PCOS, which can slow your body's weight-loss ability. When you're on keto and don't lose weight–here's 6 mistakes you can make with the Keto diet as well as how to fix it.

1. Trying to cut Carbs & Increasing Fat Too Rapidly

If you're coming from a vegetarian/vegan background or used to eat cereal in breakfast, sandwiches in lunch & pasta in dinner. EASE yourselves into carb restriction. Determining to get on the keto bandwagon & consuming the required 20-25 grams of carbs a day can wreak havoc on the body. An average apple has 25 grams of carbs, for reference. And if you've consumed more than 200 grams of carbs a day, your body will rebel and give off symptoms like the flu. When you're new to keto, suggest a weekly tapering of your carb intake. For instance: if you consume 200 g of carbs per day: start with 100-150 g of carbs a day and taper down by 25 g per week. Ok, you're not going to get straight into "ketosis," but you're going to start building up a lower carbohydrate tolerance. In the longer term, taking small steps to raise your existing carb intake will function more in your benefit.

2. Not taking pre-existing or underlying health conditions into account

Do you suffer from chronic health issues such as adrenal exhaustion, inflammatory, or thyroid problems? The origins of these disorders are a consequence of hormonal imbalance. Women's ketosis is tricky, as food, climate, and sleep changes could all have a huge impact on your hormones. When your sex hormones become out of control, the overall targets for health & weight loss will be affected. Consult your doctor first to test your hormones.

For example: By measuring the thyroid hormone levels in your blood, your doctor may diagnose hyperthyroidism/hypothyroidism. Such tests assess both the thyroid hormones themselves and the thyroid-stimulating hormone (TSH). TSH is a pituitary gland released chemical which activates your thyroid. When you know the current condition of your health, the ketogenic diet may be changed to reap the full advantages of nutritional ketosis.

3. Stressing Out so much.

Going' keto' will bring some degree of pressure on your body, as reducing carbohydrates would trigger a hunger reaction in your body. And it activates the tension hormone named cortisol while you are mind thinks it's starving. Cortisol is not really a bad thing. However, too much can lead to symptoms such as:

- Gaining weight across the mid-section.
- High blood pressure.
- Weakness in the muscles.
- Acne or dark spots.
- Menstrual cycles are irregular.

Cortisol is helpful in cases where a lion chases you (let's hope that never occurs), and you've got to run. The swift movement of action induces stress on your bodies as well as generates cortisol for such a short duration. Or if you are continually stressed by:

- long working hours.
- Motherhood Responsibilities.
- Not having a sufficient sleep.
- Over-exercising.

- Have not eaten whole foods.
- Not eating enough.

Yet daily exposure to it. Most of those factors can lead to higher levels of stress yet cortisol in the body. In short, stress is messing with the hormones and stopping fat burning. When you suffer from either of the above-mentioned symptoms, then it is time to see your doctor.

4. Intermittent Fasting Too Soon On

Intermittent fasting may be a major addition to keto to enhance the loss of fat. As a bit of background, intermittent fasting is a time-limited diet, where you consume all your meals within a specified time span. Usually, the time period is eight hours or less. You are fasting for eighteen hours, feeding during the eight-hour period. It causes the body to use all the glycogen (glucose) contained in your muscles & liver when you fast and miss the meal. By the time glucose drops out, instead, the body will move to use fat for energy. Makes sense, right? Hang on for a bit. Fasting is indeed a hormetic stressor, which means it's a stressful contribution without food.

They noticed that female rats were less fertile in the fasting studies done on rats. While the male rats were hornier and more fertile. Of course, we aren't rodents. But it's worth mentioning that we experienced female rats: smaller ovarian sizes-not ideal for fertility. Increases the size of the adrenal gland-suggesting persistent stress. And abnormal menstrual cycles-anybody skipped the period? Women who do intermittent fasting in combination with keto will feel a higher stress level.

Start either with keto or intermittent fasting first through personal experience–NOT all at once. Why you don't lose weight on Keto-intermittent fasting so fast on. Reduce overwhelming and first make use of the keto way of eating. And move to the intermittent fasting when the body has adjusted.

It scares me when people say that in order to be in ketosis, you have to be on a "keto diet." This can result in KETOSIS being on a keto diet and doing intermittent fasting. Depending on the last moment you ate, your body will fall in and out of ketosis at various times of the day. Having said that, on intermittent fasting, some females who are already-fit, unstressed & at a healthy weight might do well. But if you're not fat-adapted, get enough sleep, alleviate stress and exercise too much or too less -you shouldn't be fasting.

5. Continuously Measuring Yourself on The Scales.

This was one of my bad habits when I started my path to lose weight. Weigh yourself every day, becoming depressed or frustrated whenever the scales do not turn. Your body weight contains bone, muscle mass, fluid, organs, un-digested food, as well as the weight of body fat. Your body weight can fluctuate every day based on how much water and food you have consumed in the daytime. The number shown on the scale isn't an indicator of how much fat you have or your health. You may probably have a half kilo of feces and water to be excreted. It's not about your fat; this just means you have to go to the bathroom.

If you want regular and observable results: Weigh ONCE a week on a similar day. After using your toilet, weigh yourselves in the morning.

Weigh yourselves without shoes, so just put your knickers on. Decide a day you didn't eat excessively the previous night. If you plan on dining out on the weekend, Friday morning works. Set an alert for the weekly weighs in on your mobile phone. Report your weight to a newspaper or health app, and then cover your weekly scales.

6. Exercising So Hard Early On.

Being in Ketosis increases energy efficiency When you've adjusted to it. Fat & ketones are a perfect source of energy but are emitted at a steady rate.

Glucose or sugar quickly offers energy, and you're expected to feel the change in the gym. When you shift into keto, during the first few weeks, you will feel tired and weak, because your body is still relying on glucose to power your training, which makes a poor idea for HIIT or intense weight exercise. Go out for a long walk instead, and carry light weights than you usually do. This could help you to keto-adapt, rather than damage your body. So, if you think you're already keto-er but don't see the weight change. Then you have to test how much you're eating, so look again at the calories. Are you over-eating? Eating at a 30 percent extreme calorie deficit? Do you eat enough to power up your workout? Or are you working too hard rising your cortisol level?

Chapter 5: Healthy lifestyle with a ketogenic diet

The ketogenic diet was initially mainly seen as an insider strategy by bodybuilders who enjoyed muscle building while successfully losing body and weight fat. If you haven't learned of the keto diet before: it's also called "anabolic diet." In this dietary regime, you mostly have to go off carbohydrates and sugar while eating plenty of proteins and, at first, fat, which might sound odd. Related to the paleo diet, you may enjoy lots of meat, eggs, cheese, some fruits and lots of vegetables, and you have to go and do goodbye kiss the pasta, noodles, potatoes, and rice. It is essential that you always eat less than, precisely 30 grams of carbs a day during the ketogenic diet. This will keep your levels of insulin down and make it seem like a significant supply bottleneck to your body–otherwise, the desirable ketogenic effect will be forfeited immediately. In the beginning, it requires up to three days really to start kicking in the full effect of the keto diet, as ketosis. That means your body is responding to the crisis and changing the way it burns oil. Less fat is retained, and more growth hormones are emitted at the same time-a a perfect tool for your training scheme. Since there are hardly any carbs to move, your body will start searching for alternative energy sources, and–yay! Seek them in fat previously-stored: ketosis: ideal fat burning support and sexercise workout.

5.1 Health benefits of a ketogenic diet

The ketogenic diet gets the credit for being such a fast way of losing weight, but studies show that this low-carb, high-fat eating strategy may have several other benefits.

Keto diet is any low-carb diet strategy that is adequate to turn the body into the development and burning state of a large number of ketones, mainly acetoacetate (AcAc), as well as its derivatives acetone & beta-hydroxybutyrate (BHB). Such molecules, particularly AcAc and BHB, are used for energy by the brain as well as other tissues and have a range of health benefits. Keto is to some, but not to others, a healthy condition. Epilepsy and other brain disorders such as Alzheimer's disease are most confirmed. For people seeking keto for weight loss or success, there are further health issues. There are records of adverse reactions to keto in people, like menstrual disturbances, gut dysbiosis, circadian rhythm shift, hair loss, constipation, anxiety disorders, and thyroid dysfunction, and insulin resistance as well as nonalcoholic fatty liver in rodents.

In regards to weight loss, one of the advantages of keto is the hunger appears to be reduced. Nutritional ketosis has been used to help prevent and kill cancer cells beyond the fat loss and the factors previously described that are linked with inflammation in the brain-body. Ketosis improves other types of cellular healing, like mitochondrial biogenesis (producing new, bigger, even higher energizing mitochondria), so the cells become stronger with more resilient, especially when it comes to workout.

For instance, some endurance & ultra-endurance athletes claim their performance increases in nutritional ketosis because they have more fat than carb reserves relative to sugar burning.

Rising Energy Level

It's not unusual for people to develop the "keto flu" in the first few days of the keto diet, a short time in which you might have headaches, tiredness, fatigue, and nausea.

All such symptoms are an indication that the body is making the transition from consuming glucose (carbon sugar) to consuming fat for energy — a process known The change will leave you feeling exhausted for a day or maybe two, however, once you get through to the fat-burning process, you will find that you have far more strength and stamina. "You can do more without hitting' the wall,' says the health and fitness specialist Carrie Burrows, Ph.D.

Protection against Type 2 Diabetes

The keto diet reduces the daily carbs to below 20 grams; this may help the people with diabetes control the disease. Year-long research showed that placing type 2 diabetic people into ketosis greatly enhanced their regulation of blood sugar. Also, Steve Phinney, MD, Ph.D., Virta Health chief medical officer reports, a type 2 diabetes reversal cure, "Patients will lose an average of 12% of their body weight, around 31 pounds."

Inflammation markers fall

Doctors can assess inflammation levels in the body through blood tests for counts of high-sensitivity C-reactive proteins (hsCRP) as well as white blood cells (WBC).

In Dr. Phinney's report, "patients recorded a 39% reduction in hsCRP and 9% reduction in white blood cells," says Dr. Phinney. "Latest findings have also been seen in a two-year study showing a 29% reduction in hsCRP adopting a low-carb diet." Dr. Phinney states that inflammation is closely associated with many different health problems, including heart disease, diabetes, autoimmune disorders, and arthritis. "It's quite likely that a whole host of problems might be changed by reducing inflammation via nutritional ketosis."

Sleeping Sounder

Most people report sleeping a lot better on a ketogenic diet, says Sheet Pan Ketogenic personal trainer & author, Pamela Ellgen.

Nonetheless, you may have insomnia or trouble staying asleep during the transition phase (the very first 3 to 5 days when you start the keto). That will stop once your body adapts to burning stored fat and ketosis. Instead, when you wake up, you may find that you might sleep longer and better, sleep deeper & feel more comfortable and restful.

Improves Heart Health

It might seem odd for the heart to have a diet packed with fats positive, but this is just what Dr. Phinney recommends. "The one-year study substantially enhanced 22 of 26 cardiovascular risks. Most significantly, these patients witnessed a mean 24% decrease in triglyceride fasting, an 18% rise in healthy HDL cholesterol, and substantial decreases in both systolic & diastolic blood pressure.

"Dr. Phinney states for all of these observations that research into the effects of keto is still in early stages. "The truth is, there are no long-term, peer-reviewed evidence linking any of these changes to nutritional ketosis yet,"

Sharper Brain

'Although sugar can be a fantastic, rapid type of energy, it doesn't maintain your brain at its best. "There's a lot of data arising out that shows the brain works on ketones more effectively than it would on blood sugar, but the study is still relatively recent," says Olin. "If glucose is not available, ketones are produced to fuel the brain," says Kristen Mancinelli, a professional dietitian & author of The Ketogenic Diet. "The brain derives 100% of its nutrition from glucose on a regular diet. Up to 2/3 of brain energy on a ketogenic diet arrives from ketones. It's obvious that brain activity on a ketogenic diet would change dramatically.

Assisting women's health

A comprehensive review released in 2013 reviewed the findings and proof of keto diets that boost fertility (it looks very promising). Research also suggests that low-carbohydrate dieting can help effectively treat Polycystic Ovary Syndrome (PCOS), which decreases or removes signs such as rare or prolonged menstrual cycles, acne & obesity. Overall, maintaining low and stable levels of blood sugar, resulting in lower insulin levels in the blood, helps to regulate as well as stabilize other levels of hormones, particularly in women. Naturally, this has downstream advantages on a wide variety of insulin-related metabolic processes, such as hunger & energy consumption.

Helping the eyes

Like every diabetic would tell you, elevated blood sugar is very well known to have a negative impact on your eyesight and contribute to a higher risk for cataracts. Therefore, it is not shocking that maintaining low levels of blood sugar enhances eye & vision safety, as a gazillion persons have posted on the internet, and research on related diabetes has proven.

Muscle gain and endurance enhancement

In particular, BHB has been used to promote muscle production. Merged with plenty of anecdotal proof over the years, there's a whole trend around bodybuilders that uses a ketogenic strategy to achieve more muscle and far less fat (usually muscle gain often occurs with fat gain, so the appropriate focus is provided to avoiding this). Dr. Stephen Phinney & Dr. Jeff Volek have both written a number of articles on keto dieting for super-endurance athletes. In short, when these athletes are completely fat-adapted, there has been evidence to indicate that over and above a "natural" carb-rich diet, physical and mental performance is dramatically improved.

Controlling diabetes, obesity, & metabolic syndrome while sparing muscle loss

Of course, with the word's "diabetes" and "ketosis" or "ketogenic" in the title alone, there have been over 160 research articles currently on Pubmed. It is beyond doubts that a ketogenic diet is highly successful for many people with type I as well as type II diabetes for all of the above-mentioned reasons linked to keeping blood sugar & insulin in check.

Moreover, recent studies on the impact of a keto diet on obesity over the past few years suggest that it is an incredibly successful way not only to lose weight but also to spare muscle loss whereas curbing many obesity-related disorders (many of which were discussed above), such as the collection of symptoms & risk factors identified as Metabolic Syndrome.

5.2 Easy and quick recipes to follow

For those of you who have chosen to buy the audiobook, the recipes mentioned here are attached in a PDF file that'll help you in adopting the healthy lifestyle.

At first, a keto diet could sound daunting. But don't worry-the the easier it gets, the more you know. Eating keto might become part of the routine by prepping meals, in advance preparing your meals, and keeping a list of simple recipes for reference. Below, you'll dive into hints, tricks & recipes for keto. But first, the fundamentals of a keto diet are quickly recaptured here. The ketogenic diet puts the body in ketosis: burning of fat (instead of carbs) for energy. Ketosis offers a variety of health benefits, including loss of weight as well as cognitive benefits. Keto is a low-carbohydrate diet with high-fat content. Following these macronutrient recommendations, most people will reach ketosis:

- 70-80 percent of calories will derive from fat.
- Protein will make up 20-25 percent of calories.
- Carbohydrates will account for 5-10 percent of calories.

You can only eat 30 grams of total carbs on a ketogenic diet. This "starves" the carbohydrate system, which would otherwise be transformed into hepatic glucose. Without any glucose available, the body uses ketones as its main source of energy, turning the body into a state of fat burning.

Simple Keto Breakfasts

Keto Oatmeal.

Missing oatmeal? This keto oatmeal requires 5 minutes to cook, and only requires 3 steps. It's also filled with fats, protein, as well as fiber of 16 grams.

Savory Crustless Breakfast Keto Quiche.

What is the toughest part of quiche-making? Its crust. Which portion of a quiche is highest in carbs? Its crust. You prevent yourself from the carbs by preparing a crustless quiche, as well as the time & headache of baking.

Crunchy Coconut Cluster Keto Cereal.

One of the cooking activities that take the most time is cleaning up. Only two items (a baking sheet as well as a large bowl) are used in this keto cereal, saving you energy and time after boiling.

Chocolate Sea Salt Shake.

Here's a set of directions you're going to love: put all the items in a blender, mix, enjoy. This is not so any easier than just that. Plus, who does not like breakfast chocolate?

Avocado Egg Bowls.

Made with only five basic ingredients, these bowls of avocado eggs will be a staple of your home every week. Plus, they are quick to make ahead— just do double the ingredient, and store for breakfast all week in a plastic bag.

Keto Brunch Spread.

Hard boil eggs? So easy Facilities. Asparagus rolled in bacon? It's easy Facilities. A meal of 3 ingredients? Just too easy. Inspire your mates with the spread of this delicate brunch (and confuse them into believing you've been in the kitchen all morning).

Breakfast Casserole.

Casseroles are very easy, go-to meals for a variety of reasons. Firstly, they are cooked in one dish and would need little washing. Second, dividing your casserole into squares of equal size is simple, and then wrapping each cube in tin foil. Simply pick up one on the way to work every morning, then throw microwave into your office.

Easy Keto Lunches

Smoked Salmon Pate with Cucumber.

This recipe is extremely relatively easy to make for noon or as an appetizer for parties. Simply slice the fresh cucumber & layer after you have cooked your fish pate for a fast and easy recipe.

Slow Cooker -Taco Soup.

Nothing is more relaxing in the colder months than a bowl of the slow cooker taco soup. In the slow cooker, simply mix your fresh ground meat, stock, and seasonings to make a tasty meal.

Zesty Lime Chile Tuna Salad.

This simple salad for the tuna takes only one plate and two measures. In a large bowl, simply combine all the ingredients, then pour over your favorite salad or lettuce for a fast lunch.

Easy White Turkey Chili.

The white turkey chili contains just eight ingredients. The low-carbohydrate cauliflower rice is switched in here, and the legumes are omitted for a simple, low-carb lunch.

Sheet Pan Brussels Sprouts and Bacon.

For this recipe, here's what you need: Brussels sprouts, salt, bacon, and pepper. This is it. For a go-to daily lunch, roast on some kind of sheet pan at 400 ° F for 35 minutes.

30-Minute Spicy Keto Ramen Bowl

Sure, it is likely that ramen is safe. Yeah, it can be keto ramen. This ramen dish tastes so much better than the things you've been heating up in college, and that it's ready in 30 minutes.

Keto Cauliflower Mac & Cheese

The only thing simpler than this mac & cheese recipe is the things you can find in a box, with only eight ingredients. Furthermore, this variant is much safer, replacing carb-loaded macaroni noodles to low-carb cauliflowers. Enjoy it by yourself or as a safe side dish.

Easy Keto Dinners

Baked Pork Chops

Apart from pork chops & Parmesan cheese, seasoning is all you require for this easy dinner. It takes only 10 minutes of cooking time, then throws 50 minutes in the oven and bake.

Quick Keto Egg Roll in a Bowl.

Buying a rotisserie chicken is a simple, time-saving idea, shredding it and using it in different recipes. Mix shred chicken and slaw, and season for a fast weekend dinner here.

Ultra-Simple Chicken Cauliflower Fried Rice.

The new product used to display the aisle of produce? Fully prepared-riced cauliflower.

Save time and trouble in a food processor grating cauliflower & pick up a riced cauliflower bag for this simple, Asian-inspired dish.

Spicy Beef Keto Fajitas.

Simply slice the bell peppers, onion & strip steak for a simple taco Tuesday. Then mix to a fast dish with spice in a skillet.

Prep-Ahead Low-Carb Casserole.

Are you on weeknights crunched for a moment? Start preparing this casserole on Sunday night, then throw into the oven on Monday, when you do get home from work. Plus, leftovers will be there— sufficient to get you via several dinners.

Enchilada-Style Stuffed Peppers.

Stuffed chilies are one of the most quickly made recipes. Simply sauté the vegetables and meat in a skillet, stuff the chilies then put them in the oven. Switch out the seasonings, swapping Mexican spices for Italian, using the very same formula for two separate meals.

BBQ Pulled Beef Sando.

The slow cooker is an excellent device in trying to save money and time. Mix all components in the slow cooker in this pulled beef recipe & cook for 10 to 12 hours. You can place the ingredients overnight and get them prepared by morning, or cook them when you wake up and they're ready to get out of work.

Brown Butter Buffalo Bites.

If you're a fan of Monday's meatless, you may want to try some buffalo bits. They only need five items, 10 minutes of preparation time, and about 20 minutes of cooking time. Appreciate as a weekly dinner or an appetizer appealing to the crowd.

Savory Keto Stir Fry, Shrimp.

Stir-fries are extremely quick to prepare meals, need very few total carbs as well as typically need only one skillet. Plus, packaged vegetables (as well as, surprisingly, frozen seafood) work well in stirring fry recipes. Buy a bag of frozen vegetables and hold on hand— you'll be able to cook a delicious meal, even if you're unable to go shopping.

Low-Carb Crispy Keto "Fried" Chicken.

Want a simple recipe for the keto fried chicken? Seasoning, crushed nuts, chicken thighs or breasts, a Ziploc container, and a baking tray are everything you need. Bake it in oven for about 30 minutes, and have a dinner of soul food that seemed too great to be safe.

Mushroom Bacon Skillet.

This basic, week-end meal comprises only five items. Only add bacon, mushrooms & seasonings over medium to high heat in a skillet. Marinate for 10 mins, and have a single-pot meal for yourself.

5.3 Tips for women to achieve success

Now that we have fundamentals of keto covered, let's get into how women trying to attain a ketosis state can differ. I believe the keto diet is still too ignored as a way to treat females-specific health issues; it may need to be done differently to see results. You could benefit, as a woman, from a keto diet if you:

- Have PCOS.
- Have periods that are abnormal or absent.
- Have Thyroid hormones imbalanced.
- Depending on what you do, you can't lose out or gain weight.
- Get frightful PMS.
- Get adrenal tiredness.
- Feel exhausted or unwell.
- Feel hangry, so still have to have a convenient snack among meals.
- Want to improve your gym results.
- Have had an autoimmune disorder that you want to treat.

Did you feel ready to make the shift yet? Let's think about how YOU should make it work.

4 Success Tips

Take this one slow. Any reason to go from eating your normal diet to becoming keto the next day. Having a 3-4 week shift in macros will ensure that you maintain your body healthy and stress-free.

Also, when people take a new diet, it surprises the body so far that it places even more of a strain on our bodies, leaving us in a weakened state of adrenal control and increased output of cortisol. We may eliminate the inevitable stressor that it will create by allowing the body the space to adapt for many weeks. In the Fat Burn Female Project, we gradually change our week-by-week macronutrient proportions for four weeks monitoring method until we arrive safely and efficiently at the desired keto ratios.

Don't go zero carb. No need to remove a whole macronutrient. While we don't actually have NEED carbs for survival, because our liver generates all the glucose that we need every day, it's also needless to convince yourself that carbs are bad or you can't have them. Those kinds of constraints we place on food eventually contribute to overeating, unhealthy eating, and disappointment feelings. It is not your usual "fast fix" diet, so you don't even need to go there. Some people do well at the upper end of the ketosis scale of carbohydrates.

It may be linked to the additional supply of glucose, or it could just be because carbs make them happy, and happiness causes healing! The benefit of women's keto diets is that they can be versatile. You will find out what functions for you, the body, and the health needs you need. Getting your carbohydrate tolerance found once in ketosis is very easy. You can use either a blood ketone detector and test strips, or a Ketonix breathalyzer meter if you want to test for it.

When you get a good reading that you're in ketosis, you can play with various ratios of macronutrients to see how long you can remain within the range. If it does not sound like a good idea to buy another contraction, you could use the intuition to direct you to ketosis. Once you encounter the difference in energy levels, mental focus, and appetite, you will go by what you feel and remember. Those are clear indicators of being in ketosis. In there, take note as to how you have felt after putting in some carbs because you might have had too much, so you don't have those amazing feelings.

Let go of your fat worry as well as diet mentality. That is the big reason women would need to treat the keto diet differently. We discovered for most of us somewhere on the way that fat became bad, made up weight gain, and triggered health problems. There's plenty of research and evidence to prove the very opposite, but it can be difficult to change our minds! The only way the system works is to get over the mindset of the diet, the belief that the "calories-in must be less than out for weight loss," and all the other misconceptions of the last few decades. Instead, view it with the health-gain mindset. Know that dietary fat is the essential nutrient at work for cell-repair, building hormones, supplying and consuming nutrients, and so much more. If wellbeing is at the center of every action you take, the body has no other choice than delivering. And THAT is key.

It's not a low food diet. Some of the healthcare community's biggest myths are that low carbohydrate diets can be unhealthy and ineffective. In a way, I understand.

When you minimize your carbs but don't make up for such food by raising your consumption of fat, otherwise, the diet is far too low in calories, nutrients, and energy, and of course, nothing good can come out of it! Note, it's a very HIGH FAT, low-carb diet, and not a low-carb diet. That is nothing but a disaster.

Here are some more effective tips:

1. Start preparing your home for Keto progress.

It's essential to get ready for that before you start a new eating program. Get ahead of the banned foods and store the Keto-friendly choices in your kitchen. If you're a "snack stasher," don't forget to clean out those places too–your bag, your bedside table, back of the refrigerator where ice cream is concealed from the baby.

2. Plan ahead.

Now's the time to implement meal preparation. Anyway, it's a wonderful idea but more so when you start a new eating plan. Prepare as far as possible of your snacks and meals ahead of time. It will allow you to stop the feeling of "nothing to eat" at the last minute and also to allow you with your shopping list.

3. Gain knowledge of your portion sizes.

With time, you're going to get a feeling for the right portion sizes, but meanwhile, a kitchen scale, as well as a decent set of measuring cups & spoons, are a perfect way to make sure you don't over-eat.

4. Use a daily food journal.

Report your average meal intake in a newspaper. Not only is this a smart way to ensure you're on track for performance, but it's also a tremendous motivator.

If you have a hard time adhering to your diet schedule, just take a look back at some of your good days before.

5. Make a Keto buddy.

When you adopt a new eating plan, it is so essential to have help. It may be a member of your family or a buddy who is eager to join you in a Keto diet program. Cheer one another, share your obstacles and achievements, and provide one another tips and ideas for the recipe!

6. Find Keto-friendly alternative options when eating out.

When cooking for yourself at home, many individuals find it relatively easy to get in the groove of this new diet program. This is eating out, which is becoming a problem. Check the menu online if you're going to a restaurant, particularly one that's new to you. Before you go, get an idea of the meal options, so you don't get confused once you get into it.

7. Maintain your levels of stress.

Stress may affect the efficiency of a Ketogenic diet program. You need to sleep enough, get into some physical exercise every day, and find some fun ways of reducing your stress. Mindfulness, warm baths, relaxation, fun trips, sports, and other recreational activities are all successful ways to deal with stress.

8. Find certain yummy Keto recipes & then use them.

A Keto diet is so popular at the moment now, and there are lots of websites out there with tasty Keto recipes. Lots of them you will find at Pinterest. Everything you need to do is look. Collecting a list of delicious-sounding Keto-friendly meals is a perfect way to keep your eating plan inspired.

9. Be sure you're consuming sufficient fiber as well as fat.

Most of us get the bulk of our fiber through high carb foods such as whole grains, which makes it a struggle to get enough on a keto diet.

When you are sure to get plenty of your carbohydrates from non-starchy veggies like kale, broccoli, Brussels sprouts, spinach, cauliflower, & cabbage, it's always probable to have the fiber you want.

10. Be ready for the "Keto flu."

When your body has been used to loads of sugar and carbohydrates, an adaptation period is expected to occur after you have started implementing a Keto diet. It's usually referred to as "keto flu," with symptoms such as dizziness, nausea, concentration trouble, stomach pain, cramping, even sleeping difficulties.

Many of the suggestions already mentioned here might help with symptoms of Keto flu, but making sure that you remain well-hydrated is still very important. Many people find it can be good to apply a bit of salt to a liter of water to cope with their effects too.

5.4 women's experiences with a ketogenic diet

Among the most famous — and controversial— diets in recent memory to sweep the lifestyle scene is the keto diet. This eating plan is low-carbon and high-fat and also can help you lose weight like crazy, but it also triggers extreme cravings, hormonal changes, mood swings, and is something profoundly unpleasant called "keto flu." The diet functions by cutting out carbohydrates and sugar, rapidly replenishing the body's energy reserves, and pushing it to find new sources of food that will be better for the nervous system and brain. The body begins producing ketones at a higher rate through eating a diet rich in the fats found naturally such as coconut oil, almonds, avocado & fatty fish. When the bloodstream contains enough ketones, you reach a metabolic state known ketosis (the actual goal of those in the keto diet), in which the body burns fat, but not muscle.

Here are the experiences of some women have adopted a keto diet:

1. "My husband and I hopped on the keto train about four months before our wedding. Associated with regular workouts, we also shed the pounds, lost some weight, felt great, and were overall super happy with the results! Now we don't fully abide by it as neither of us felt it would be sustainable in the long run, but we still follow some of the guidelines, not strictly, that we felt benefited most to each of us.

2. "I think it would be important to get a different outlook than' everything is fine, my life is awesome plus I lost 100 pounds.'" Keto brought me an endless period of time, going for weeks now. It returns in full force every time it is almost gone. This never existed before. "It's' normal' when I read about it, that fat cells shrink and release hormones. Well, I don't feel I'm losing weight. I don't like to waste my time measuring each milligram of micronutrients while counting calories to work. I'm tired and sick of vomiting and not allowing myself to give in to cravings just to be abused by my body for sticking to the diet. I believed, but I can't say that I am less than discouraged. Not going to give up yet but I feel crazier about doing this every day." — Anonymous.

3. "I adopted keto diet last year for about four months. I brought it together with fasting. During that time frame, I lost approximately eight pounds. 3 It should be noted that I exercised for 30 mins six days a week as well: 3 days for strength training & 3 days of exercise on alternating days (run/walk intervals on the treadmill). "But as soon as I started to eat starchy carbs and vegetables, I gained nearly all that was lost." — Robyn

4. "I tried keto with my husband back in August. He enjoyed it and asked me if we could go back on it, and I loved it too, however. it was a terrible experience." The reason I went to keto in the first place was that I tried to figure out what made my body feel miserable whatever I ate, and yes, I went to my doctor and get this checked. Previously I cut out all meats (not all at the same period), all dairy or even gluten, but without luck. It was not until I attempted keto that I knew that I had a high carbohydrate intolerance, which included sugar. That was perfect because I discovered exactly what caused my issues, and I turned to all meats too. I completely forgot, however, that I was hypoglycemic (because I was diagnosed as a child as well as unintentionally made it part of my lifestyle). "So keto was awesome, but only if it helped me to understand a health issue that prompted me to go to my doctor and focus on keeping a nutrition plan set up to help control low blood sugar while also eliminating the carbohydrates from my diet." — Daniela

5. "I'm a person who lost all my additional weight on keto, and I'm retaining it now. I've got PCOS, and that is possibly the best cure for it. My doctor said she needed everyone to stop sugar for that." Other big changes I've mostly been through ovulation and periods.

Rather than my period occurring a little every day for months or not occurring for months at all, it now occurs once in a month for about four days, which is perfect and' appropriate.' "Even now, I really can tell if I'm ovulating. I don't think I even ovulated before. I had been told that it was unlikely I'd ever get pregnant, however, attempting to suffocate the ovarian cysts down easily has definitely caused all kinds of ovulation signs." The worst part was getting all sentimental before my period.

I didn't have mood swings... but I do now. "The advantage was quick weight loss. I lost 50 lbs. in 4 months eating 1300 calories a day & never being starving, and doing 18/6 fasting, that I still do. I just don't track my calories as much now, but I remain between 1200-1600." Eliminated a lifetime of acne too." — anonymous.

6. "Women must be far more mindful of their calorie consumption. It is painful at times whenever I see images of the stuff that people eat on that diet. We actually can't eat lbs. of bacon, avocados, cheese loads, etc. As they're too rich in calories. If you're trying to remain at 1300 calories, just a few tablespoons of cream is 1/6 of your day's calories. That's not a good way of getting the nutrients. For a specific reason, we can't go nuts with all of the Superfoods so many Keto'ers love — almond flour baked goods, halo top ice cream, and so on. One serving of those things is really high in calories, which takes away from the proteins, vegetables, and fats we have to get. Some women find themselves in trouble with enough of their fat and protein originating from nuts and milk and not enough meat. All of that can be compared to stalls." — anonymous.

Conclusion

A keto diet is well recognized as a low-carb diet, in which the body produces ketones in the liver for energy use. It's referred to in several different terms–ketogenic diet, low carb diet or low carb high fat (LCHF), etc. If you consume something high in carbohydrates, glucose and insulin are created throughout your body. Glucose is the simplest molecule the body can manipulate and use as energy to choose it over some other source of energy. Insulin is created by taking it all over the body to absorb the glucose in your bloodstream. Since the glucose has been used as a primary energy, fats are not required and are therefore stored. Usually, the body would use glucose as the main source of energy on a regular, higher carb diet. The body is driven to a state known as ketosis by reducing the intake of carbs.Ketosis is a normal process which the body initiates to help us survive when there is a low intake of food. We develop ketones during this state, which are formed from the degradation of fats in the liver. A well-managed keto diet's end goal is to push the body into that metabolic state. They do so not by calorie deprivation but through carbohydrate starvation. Our bodies are extremely adaptable to what you put in it–when you overwhelm it with fats and remove carbohydrates, ketones will continue to be burnt as the primary source of energy. The optimum ketone rates provide several benefits in terms of health, losing weight, mental and physical performance.

To begin a ketogenic diet, you will also want to plan ahead. That means getting a viable diet plan ready. What you consume depends on how easily you want to reach a ketogenic state (ketosis).

The more restrictive you're on your carbs (less than 25 g of net carbohydrates a day), the quicker you'll get ketosis. You want to reduce your carbs, mainly from fruits, nuts, and dairy items. Should not eat processed carbs like wheat (cereal, pasta, bread), starch (beans, potatoes, legumes), or berries. The only exceptions to this are avocado, star fruit, and moderately consumable berries. Ketosis is common and even beneficial to women. Ketosis helps people with metabolic disorders such as obesity, and also PCOS. Ketosis allows them to lose extra body fat and enhance metabolism functioning, which in effect regulates female hormones. Females who are especially pregnant, underweight, lose weight quickly, or fail to consume enough fats on a keto diet to suffer menstrual disorders. It is because the formation of female sex hormones is a function of body fat & diet. Luckily, there have been ways to fix the issue. A common misunderstanding is that the keto diet is more costly than other diets. And while it might be a little more costly than buying grain-filled food, it's much better than people believe. The keto diet has specific effects on the body and within the cells, providing benefits that go beyond what some other diet can bring. The mixture of carbohydrate restriction, as well as ketone output, decreases insulin levels, activates autophagy, increases the development and efficiency of mitochondria, reduces inflammation & burns fat. This wide range of results offers a multitude of benefits with a number of different goals as well as health issues for a host of different individuals. Ultimately, eating a high amount of fat, moderate protein, and a small number of carbohydrates can have a huge effect on your health-reducing your cholesterol, body weight, blood sugar, and increasing your energy & mood rates. In the start, a ketogenic diet could be difficult to understand, but it's not as hard as it's been made out to be. The change can be a little difficult, but the clean eating movement's increasing popularity makes it easier & easier to find low-carb foods convenient.

References

What's a ketogenic diet? (n.d.). Retrieved from WebMD: **https://www.webmd.com/diet/ss/slideshow-ketogenic-diet**

A complete guide to ketosis. (n.d.). Retrieved from DietDoctor: **https://www.dietdoctor.com/low-carb/ketosis**

Ketosis for women- Does keto affect female harmones? (n.d.). Retrieved from kissmyketo: **https://www.kissmyketo.com/blogs/health/ketosis-for-women-does-keto-affect-female-hormones**

Types of ketogenic diet. (n.d.). Retrieved from Diabetes.co.uk: **https://www.diabetes.co.uk/keto/types-of-ketogenic-diet.html**

Health benefits of ketogenic dieting. (n.d.). Retrieved from KetoSchoool: **https://ketoschool.com/the-43-health-benefits-of-ketogenic-dieting-in-addition-to-weight-loss-1e4ee4743f1f**

Keto for women-How to do it right and loss weight? (n.d.). Retrieved from Perfect keto: **https://perfectketo.com/keto-for-women/**

Which keto diet you should use? (n.d.). Retrieved from Ruled.me: **https://www.ruled.me/3-ketogenic-diets-skd-ckd-tkd/**

Why is Keto diet good for you? (n.d.). Retrieved from Medical News Today: **https://www.medicalnewstoday.com/articles/319196#7-improves-pcos-symptoms**

25 recepies to keep keto simple. (n.d.). Retrieved from Perfect keto: **https://perfectketo.com/how-to-keep-it-simple-on-the-keto-diet/**

30 days ketogenic diet plan. (n.d.). Retrieved from Ruled.me: https://www.ruled.me/30-day-ketogenic-diet-plan/